Introduction

Americans are going overseas in a steady stream. Many are tourists for whom Paris, Tokyo, Bangkok and even Bombay are just their latest in a long series of conquests. Like the venerable motive to climb the mountain "because it is there," the urge to see more and more of the world's great sights and cities is compelling and rewarding.

Others Americans will be staying longer. Theirs is the sobering challenge to move into another cultural setting and to establish both home and work in a strange and often perplexing situation. These are the Expatriates for whom this book is written for.

No one who has lived overseas will tell you that it is easy. All sorts of tasks, many of them not very interesting, are involved. Worse, there are some emotional jolts along the way as you bid goodbye to friends, the familiar, and the handy. It hits hardest when you realize you have to start virtually all over again with many parts of your life: sorting out new people, establishing new friendships, and caring for family members whose own needs have changed.

The veterans of overseas service have their favorite horror stories, and part of the ritual is to pass these along to the newcomer. The tax challenges have often been a part of these horror stories as the newcomer finds out that the information that he had been given in the past was either totally wrong or incomplete.

Careful thinking about what is involved may raise the flag of caution. Any move is hard: the overseas move is one of the very hardest. The mistake about the tax laws involved for expatriates can be both costly and embarrassing. Coupled with all the other transition challenges such as shift in career pattern and lifestyle, it can be the mistake of a lifetime!

Those who want to make the overseas experience the highlight of a lifetime are invited to read, reflect, plan and prepare armed with the information in this book to be well informed on all the tax implications of living overseas.

The capacity to turn the exotic into the meaningful, the strange into the familiar, and the mysterious into the enjoyable takes good intentions, good advice, and lots of practice. There are still, attitudes to nurture, and ways to get help in the preparation process.

The reader will find in this book a reassuring tone that says, "You can make it." Scaring people into foreign expatriate tax compliance is out of style. the task today development of new skill and/or realizing that you can no longer keep abreast of the whole expatriate tax situation, and can no longer prepare your own return as you have for years in the past and realize you need the help of a tax professions who is well versed in all the intricacies of expatriate laws.

THE TAX BOOK for US EXPATS

By

Dan E. Gordon

US Income Tax Preparer

Published by Ichiban International Publishing

http://ichibaninternational.net

© 2013 Ichiban International Publishing

All rights reserved. No part of this publication may be reproduced or distributed in any form or by any means, or stored in a database or retrieval system, without the prior written permission of the publisher.

The information provided in this publication is for educational purposes only, and does not necessarily reflect all laws, rules, or regulations for the tax year covered. This publication is designed to provide accurate and authoritative information concerning the subject matter covered, but it is sold with the understanding that the publisher is not engaged in rendering legal, accounting, or other professional services. If legal advice or other expert assistance is required, the services of a competent professional person should be sought.

IRS Circular 230 Disclosure: Pursuant to the requirements of the Internal Revenue Service Circular 230, we inform you that, that to the extent any advice relating to a Federal tax issue is contained in the communication, it was not written or intended to be used, and cannot be used, for the purpose of (a) avoiding any tax related penalties that may be imposed on you or any other person under the Internal Revenue Code, or (b) promoting, marketing or recommending to another person any transaction or matter addressed in the communication.

Table of Contents

INTRODUCTION	3
GENERAL OVERVIEW OF EXPATRIATE TAX ISSUES	5
WHY FILE A US TAX RETURN	7
STATUTE OF LIMITATIONS	10
TAX PERSON	11
CITIZEN BASED TAXATION	13
GREEN CARD HOLDERS	14
EXPAT TAX OBLIGATIONS	18
MINIMUM FILING REQUIREMENTS	22
EARNED VS. UNEARNED INCOME	24
FOREIGN INCOME EXCLUSION	26
FOREIGN HOUSING EXCLUSION	34
BONAFIDE RESIDENCE TEST	36
BONAFIDE RESIDENCE PRECAUTIONS	38
PHYSICAL PRESENCE	41
FOREIGN SPOUSE	43
ITIN NEW RULES	46
DOUBLE TAXATION	48
FOREIGN TAX CREDIT	49
FAQ	51
FBAR	57
FBAR - FAQ.	60
FATCHT & FORM 8938	63
ASSET DISCLOSURE OVDI	67
PFIC INVESTMENT CO.'S	69
STATE TAXES LIABILITY	72
REQUIRED DOCUMENTS	74
TAX BRACKET	77
IRA RULES	79
PAST RETURN COPIES	81
E-FILING YOUR RETURN	82
TAX REFUNDS	83
ONLINE TAX PAYMENTS	85
ALTERNATIVE MINIMUM TAX	86
IRS NOTICES	87
IRS PENALTIES	89
AMENDED RETURNS	92
IRS AUDITS	94
THE IRS LONG ARM	97
EXPATRIATE TAX SITUATION ANALYZED	99
RESIDENT NON AND CITIZENS	110
IRS DUE DATE & DEADLINES	112
RECORD RETENTION RULES	115

General Overview of Expatriate Tax Issues

If you're planning a move abroad, or you're already an expatriate, you have more to think about than adjusting to a new culture. Although it may be tempting, you must not ignore your U.S. taxes.

Every U.S. citizen, - regardless of whether they are living in the U.S. or not, - must file a tax return with the federal government.

The tax situation for expatriates is often complicated and frustrating. Many variables affect how much expatriates pay Uncle Sam - from whether you deduct your foreign taxes, to your host country, to your employment situation.

U.S. Taxes for Expatriates - Pitfalls and Traps

To ensure a smooth tax-filing process, you must be well informed. If you take up residence in a foreign country without exploring the tax ramifications, you may find yourself paying more than you expected to the U.S. government or your home state - as well as penalties and interest.

Some of the important considerations include...

Amount of foreign earned income: You can deduct a substantial amount in earned foreign income from your U.S. taxes by filing the proper forms.

Your host country: Many countries have tax treaties or conventions with the United States, which will dictate how you file your U.S. taxes.

Which state you most recently lived in: Some states do not have income taxes; others make it difficult to sever your ties with that state. Your Expat Tax Preparer can help there also.

Rental income and dividends/interest from assets in the U.S.: You must pay taxes on these exactly as if you were living in the U.S.

Whether you are self-employed or not: You must pay *self-employment* tax on your income, even if you can exclude it as foreign earned income on your *income taxes*.

Your holdings in a foreign bank account: Any interest in or authority over a foreign financial account over a certain amount must be reported to the U.S. Treasury Department.

Although the IRS offers numerous deductions, credits, and exclusions to expats, taking advantage of them is not straightforward.

Some exclusions vary by country, while others can only be claimed for a portion of the year. In addition, each requires supporting forms and worksheets, which can be more than cumbersome to prepare.

For people who are either planning a move or have already settled abroad, a competent expat tax preparer will offer the following tax services:

U.S. Tax Returns - Prepare your U.S. income tax return, including all schedules and forms that may be required.

State Tax Returns - Depending on which state you most recently lived in, you, may need to file a state return.

Small Business Tax Returns – Your preparer should be able to assist small business owners, self-employed individuals, or folks with significant rental property with their returns.

Online Filing - When you're living in a foreign country, it's not practical to send forms and documents back and forth through the mail. Your preparer should have a highly secure; fully encrypted Client Portal that enables the quick, free, and safe transfer of files between his office and you.

Foreign Bank Account Reporting – Your preparer should be able to file the FBAR form for individuals who had above a certain threshold in a foreign account.

Compliance - It's not uncommon for expats to fall behind on their taxes. Your preparer should be able help you sort through the paperwork, forms, and rules, and get you back in compliance with the IRS.

Consulting - If you're unsure of your need to file federal or state tax returns then, give your preparer a call. Your preparer should be happy to help you get clear on your situation.

Why File A US Tax Return

- First and foremost, it's the law - If you are a U.S. citizen or resident alien, you must report income from all sources within and outside of the U.S. It's that simple. *Whether or not you end up paying tax on that income is irrelevant - the income itself must be reported*. Additionally there are five more reasons that actually make filing U.S. Tax Return advantageous to you:
- If you fail to file, you cannot claim foreign income exclusion and you may be liable for penalties.
- There is a three year statute of limitations on filed tax returns. If you do not file, the statute of limitations never runs out. Therefore it is in your interest to file to 'run the clock' and not leave yourself exposed to an audit down the road.
- Many U.S. Citizens, expats, never actually have to pay anything to the IRS - the combination of taxes paid in the host country and various deductions available to expats most often results in no taxes due the IRS, BUT you MUST file.
- If you are a green-card holder, filing U.S. tax return establishes "good moral character" in the eyes of INS USCIS for immigration compliance.
- If you do owe taxes to the IRS and do not file a return, you are liable to pay penalties and interest, which accrue in perpetuity. After about five years, the amount of penalties accrued may be more than double the original tax bill (compare it with stock market performance, which is flat for the last 10 years).

Additionally:

- The U.S. government is actively exploring the option of refusing renewal of US passports for delinquent taxpayers. Congress requested a study by the Government Accountability Office (GAO) to look into whether withholding US passports from individuals with outstanding tax balances would increase IRS tax collections. The study (http://www.gao.gov/htext/d11272.html), released by the GAO in March 2011, suggests billions in unpaid tax revenue could be claimed by the IRS if individuals owing taxes were denied US passports.
- As federal deficits continue to mount, the federal government has a vital interest in efficiently and effectively collecting the billions of dollars of taxes owed under current law. Federal law already allows the linkage of debt collection with the passport issuance process in certain areas, including for certain outstanding State Department debt and child support enforcement, the report said.
- As you have probably heard, the US government has started to actively pursue its citizens who have unreported foreign bank accounts. Congress has passed numerous laws that make it a criminal offense with draconian fines and even a threat of a jail sentence. IRS allows US citizens to come clean and report these foreign accounts under either the quiet disclosure or an occasional Offshore Voluntary Disclosure Initiative. However - whichever program you follow, you must declare that all your past due tax returns are filed.
- The US government is actively working with foreign countries that have large numbers of US expats in order to secure information about them: including; Canada, Israel and Switzerland.

- If you happen to live in different country, it is only a matter of time before they will get there. Ultimately the graph below presents all the information you need to know. US debt is exploding and the government is doing all it can to improve collection.
- The government knows that over 6 million Americans are living abroad and only, approximately, 500,000 of those file income tax returns. Their goal is to increase that number by any means.
- These are the reasons why American Expats should file US tax return.
- But what if you have left the U.S. shores years ago and don't plan on coming back?
- Let's examine the following scenarios which may apply to you or your loved ones: We have established that you are not abroad for a year or two on a business assignment, but have moved permanently and have no intention of returning to the U.S. Should you still file your U.S tax return? Are you at risk of any repercussions for failure to file? If you don't file, how will the IRS find you? Below we lay out a few situations that we have observed.
- You are an expat and get hitched to a non U.S citizen in the country you currently reside. After your honeymoon, you want to introduce your new spouse to your family and visit them in the US. Without filing federal tax returns, this may be difficult. In order for your spouse to obtain a U.S visa, you must submit copies of tax returns for the last 3 years.
- After living abroad (and not filing a tax return) for years, you switch jobs and decide to come back to the U.S. What do you tell the IRS once you begin filing again? How will you remain in good tax standing and avoid being flagged by the IRS in the future? Look at it from the perspective of the IRS. You have been M.I.A for years and they have no record of what you did for money or where you were employed.
- Your hard work paid off and you have done well for yourself while abroad. Hopefully, you don't stuff your wealth in your mattress and instead you look to invest your earnings in the largest and most liquid stock market in the world - or deposit it at an American bank. How do you demonstrate where the funds came from? Unless you want the watchful eye of the U.S government upon you, it's best to have paperwork prepared.
- Along the same vein, let's imagine that you would like to return to the U.S and buy a home. How do you prove where the money came from? Will the government question whether it was obtained legally?
- The three year statute of limitations only starts counting when a tax return is filed. If you never file - the clock never starts counting and, therefore, it never runs out. In other words - there is no statute of limitations on unfiled tax returns!
- Hopefully, you've done extremely well and have amassed a great deal of wealth and would want to leave it to your relatives or various foundations. How will your descendants explain the source of their inheritance? What questions from the IRS will they have to answer? Is there a chance that they will face your non-compliance penalties and overdue taxes?
- Currently, it is not a requirement to present copies of prior years' tax returns to renew your passport. With enhanced security measures, could this be an added requirement in the future?
- Additional thoughts:
- If your child is of college age, or if you have younger children whom you would like to see enter college in the future, ideally you would be able to pass some of the financial burden onto the government by taking advantage of numerous government

assistance programs. How will you prove that you are indeed eligible for financial assistance without producing copies of your tax returns?
- Let's say you're turning 62 and after years of paying Social Security taxes you are finally able to reap it's benefits. How will you prove your eligibility without producing copies of tax returns?
- Finally, expats can exclude over $95,100.00 (2012) of foreign earned income from tax calculation. Most importantly, in order to exclude it, you first must declare it by filing a tax return. If you don't file a tax return you risk losing the exclusion. If you lose the exclusion, the IRS has the right to include it in your taxable income.
- These are just a few of the common pitfalls for U.S citizens living abroad. The risk/reward is clear for expats, all the upside is in filing your tax return and only downside can come from failing to file.

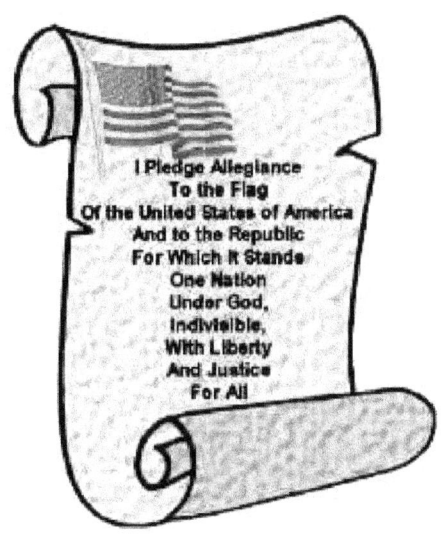

Statute of Limitations

If you do not file a tax return for a given tax year, the statute of limitations for that year never runs out. Therefore it is advisable to file a return for each year, even if your taxable income falls below the minimum amount required. This is done in order to cause the statute of limitations to run out.

If you do file your tax return each year while living abroad, the statute of limitations for IRS audits will expire three years after you file those returns. This means that the IRS cannot go back and try to audit or challenge those returns later. Therefore, you should file your return even if you have no income or do not owe taxes in order to force the statute of limitations to run out and eliminate future problems when you decide to return to the U.S.

Tax Person

All United States tax laws and regulations apply to every US Person whether he/she is working in the United States or in a foreign country. When it comes to your international tax Obligations, it's important to understand exactly how 'US Person' is defined by the IRS and what it means to you. Failure to understand your tax responsibilities as a US Person can result in hefty penalties associated with your US expat tax liability.

Who is a US Person?

Every United States Citizen.
You are liable for US income taxes whether you are a citizen who was born in the United States or outside of the United States with at least 1 parent who is a US Citizen. If you are a naturalized citizen, you are also considered a US Person.

Every United States Tax Resident.
There are 2 different methods of becoming a tax resident. One of these methods is to meet the Substantial Presence Test by having either been in the United States for at least 31 days out of 1 year or 183 days out of the 3 year period prior to the current tax year. The other method is to meet the Green Card Test; this method applies to any person who has obtained a US Green Card.

United States Citizens Born Outside of the US
If you were born outside of the United States and have dual citizenship with the US and the foreign country in which you were born, you have a different set of options – especially if you've never lived in the United States. It's important to realize, however, that – until you exercise those options – you are still considered a US Person for tax reporting purposes, and you must meet all of your US tax obligations. If you wish to voluntarily terminate your US Citizenship (http://www.us-taxman.com/Expatriationlaw.php) avoid being responsible for US taxes, you have the right to do so.

Inactive Green Card Holders
If you have never surrendered your US Green Card and your Green Card is considered to be expired by the USCIS (US Citizenship and Immigration Service) you are still obligated to file a US expat tax return every year. You will be required to file an annual US expat tax return until you either surrender your Green Card or there has been a judicial ruling that your Green Card has been abandoned or revoked. If you have ever held a Green Card in the United States and you are not sure whether or not you have any current tax liability, it will be in your best interest to find out and take care of any outstanding tax obligations.

Your Tax Obligations as a US Person
Depending on a variety of circumstances including filing status, source of income, and whether or not you can be claimed as a dependent; any US Person who earns more than the minimum threshold of around $6K-$10K dollars in a calendar year is required to file a

US income tax return. If you are living and working abroad, you are still required to file an annual US expat tax return – even if you wind up not owing any taxes.

In addition to being required to file an annual US expat tax return, you are also required to report any foreign banking or investment activity if you have an account balance of more than $10K. It's important to realize that the $10K threshold applies to all of your accounts combined. For example, if you have a foreign checking account with a balance of $5K, a savings account with $4K, and an investment account worth $2K; you will be required to report all of this activity on Form TD F 90-22.1 (http://www.us-taxman.com/fbar.php) and mail this form to the United States Department of Treasury. If you have a vested interest in any foreign corporations, partnerships, or trusts; you will be required to report this information, as well. If you have earned income from investments or interest on your foreign accounts, you must report this income on your US expat tax return.

Consequences for Ignoring Your Tax and Reporting Obligations

If your foreign income exceeds the minimum filing requirement established by the IRS and you fail to file a US expat tax return, you will be subject to a number of fines. If you wind up having owed taxes to the United States you will be assessed both a Failure to Pay Fee and a Late Payment Fee. Additionally, you will be charged interest on a daily basis until your US tax obligations are met. If you have not filed a US expat tax return for 1 or more years, we can help get you caught up with minimal fees by filing back taxes with the IRS.

If you have foreign accounts with a balance of $10K or more and you fail to report this activity to the Department of Treasury you will be subject to both a $10K fine and up to 50% of your foreign account balances. Additionally, you may have to face criminal evasion charges and potentially serve time in federal prison. If you have failed to submit Form TD F 90-22.1 for 1 or more years, you may be able to escape these hefty penalties by taking advantage of the OVDI (Offshore Voluntary Disclosure Initiative), which allows US Persons with foreign bank accounts to 'come clean' on their own accord for a guarantee of no criminal charges and reduced penalties. If you wait until the IRS tracks you down, you will not qualify for the lenient terms of the OVDI.

How Will the IRS know if I'm Earning Foreign Income or Have Foreign Accounts?

The IRS is continuously seeking new methods of identifying US taxpayers who have not met their US tax filing and reporting obligations in previous years. Not only has the IRS begun to hire more international employees to track down US tax evaders, it has also gone to greater lengths holding foreign institutions responsible for not reporting the income or banking activity of US Persons. Additionally, the United States has more than 60 active treaties with other countries in which there is an agreement to share all tax related information. For US Persons ignoring their US tax obligations, it's not a matter of IF the IRS will catch up to you; it's a matter of WHEN. If you are proactive and become compliant before the IRS tracks you down, you have a much better chance of escaping punitive charges.

Because of all the different circumstances of US Persons living and working abroad, filing a US expat tax return can get quite complicated. Your expat tax preparer should have expat tax professionals available to answer your questions and/or file a US expat tax return on your behalf.

Citizen Based Taxation

Systems of personal income tax vary enormously around the world. The differences are big and small, simple and complex. Some countries' personal income tax code consists of one word - "none" - while other countries' consist of volumes and volumes of intricate details.

However, almost all nations are unified on one point: a country only taxes non-residents on, at most, income earned within the country. Residents are fully taxed by the country according to its tax code. But if you don't live there, then your personal income tax obligation to that country is limited to, at most, tax on only the income earned within that country. This is the essence of what is called "territorial taxation".

The United States is an exception.
"The USA is one of the few countries of the world which levies personal income tax on all its citizens: not only on its residents - citizens or non-citizens - but also on its citizens who do not live in the country. All citizens of the United States are taxed under the same personal income tax system, regardless of whether they live in the country or abroad." This citizenship-based taxation is very unique. How unique?

Only the U.S. and Eritrea
Several countries tax non-residents for a short period after they move abroad. For example, an individual who leaves a country may continue to be taxed until he has been a non-resident for at least 6 months or a year. But permanent, lifelong taxation regardless of residency is extremely rare. In 1995, the U.S. Congress took (yet another) look at the situation and found that only 3 countries in the world taxed based on citizenship rather than residency: Philippines, Eritrea, and the United State. A year later, the Philippines ended its citizenship-based tax regime.

As for Eritrea, it imposes a special 2% tax on all Eritreans abroad - dual-nationals included - in order to fund the dictatorial one-party government which has ruled since independence in 1993. This is a special tax on citizens abroad, as opposed to the U.S., which imposes the same tax regime on citizens regardless of where they reside. Eritrea does not allow renunciation of citizenship, so anyone who ever was a citizen carries this tax burden his whole life.

The enforcement mechanism for the citizenship-abroad tax is simple: if you are an Eritrean citizen abroad and don't pay the special tax, then your relatives in Eritrea will be severely harassed, beaten and imprisoned. Additionally, the Eritreans abroad who don't pay the special tax are not allowed to cross the Eritrean border or are arrested when they attempt to leave Eritrea.

Interestingly, a Canadian court in Toronto ruled in 2007 that the imposition of the 2% tax on its citizens abroad was illegal and that a dual Canadian-Eritrean citizen should be paid back the money he had given.

This leaves the United States as the only country in the world which applies the same tax regime to all its citizens, regardless of where they live.

Green Card Holders

As a U.S. green card holder working abroad you may be worried about how the disclosure of the foreign earned income may affect your prospective application for U.S. citizenship. Remember your Tax Preparer is a tax specialist - not an immigration lawyer. We cannot provide specific legal advice but can still offer the following general information.

We know from our experience that filing tax return each year is extremely important for applicants seeking U.S. citizenship. Living and earning money overseas while reporting your income and paying taxes to the U.S. Treasury makes your prospects for the American citizenship much brighter than non-reporting of your income at all. You should always file a U.S. resident tax return (Federal Form 1040). You **should not file a non-resident return**, Form 1040NR; even if all of your salary and wages were earned outside the U.S.

Green card holders are considered residents of the U.S. for income tax purposes, meaning that they have to file a U.S. income tax return on their worldwide income, regardless of whether they are in the U.S. or in another country. Receiving the benefits of a green card holder (i.e. as a resident) and taking advantage of the tax laws as a non-resident alien are in conflict, and that can invalidate your green card.

Below is the link to the IRS document that provides further detail on this topic. The IRS Green Card Holders Guide for Basic Tax information is here:
(http://www.irs.gov/pub/irs-pdf/p4588.pdf). If you have a U.S. green card, you are a lawful permanent resident of the U.S. even if you live abroad. This means you are treated as a U.S. resident for U.S. income tax purposes and you are subject to U.S. tax on your worldwide income from whatever source derived. Accordingly, you must file a U.S. tax return unless **(a)** there has been a final administrative or judicial determination that your lawful permanent resident status has been revoked or abandoned, **(b)** your gross income from worldwide sources is less than the amounts that require a tax return to be filed, or **(c)** your U.S. residence status is affected by an income tax treaty.

What if my green card has been taken by or given to someone in the U.S. government?

If you've surrendered your green card, this doesn't necessarily mean that your status as a lawful permanent resident has changed. Your status will not change unless and until you get an official notice from the U.S. Citizenship and Immigration Service (USCIS) that there has been a final administrative or judicial determination that your green card has been revoked or abandoned. You can contact the USCIS to check the status of your card.

What if I have been absent from the U.S. for a long period of time?

Your tax responsibilities as a green card holder do not change if you are absent from the U.S. for any period of time. Your income tax filing requirement and possible obligation to pay U.S. taxes continue until you either surrender your green card or there has been a final administrative or judicial determination that your green card has been revoked or abandoned. Therefore, even if the U.S. Citizenship and Immigration Service (USCIS) no longer recognizes the validity of your green card because you have been absent from the United States for a certain period of time or the green card is more than ten years old, you must continue to file tax returns until there has been a final determination that is not subject to appeal that your green card has been revoked or abandoned.

What if I haven't filed prior U.S. Income Tax Returns?
If you have not filed a U.S. income tax return for one or more years and there is no tax liability for any of those years, you should file returns for the current year and two prior years. However, if you have not filed a U.S. income tax return for one or more years and income tax is due for any of those years, you should file returns for the current year and five previous years.

What if I have income taxes withheld from income I received from the U.S.?
When an entity in the U.S. makes a non-wage payment (like social security or pension payments) to a nonresident alien, it is required to withhold 30% of the payment (only 85% of a social security payment is subject to the 30% tax) and forward it to the IRS. When an entity in the U.S. sends a payment to a green card holder who lives outside the U.S., it generally should not withhold the 30% tax. If this tax is withheld in error because you have a foreign address, you should notify the payer of the income with a Form W-9 to stop the withholding and you can claim a refund of the tax withheld in error.

What if I'm living in another country? Do I have to pay taxes to both the U.S. and the country where I am living?
A green card holder is considered to be a resident of the U.S. for U.S. income tax purposes and is therefore subject to U.S. taxes on worldwide income. If there is no income tax treaty between your country of residence and the U.S., you must pay taxes to both countries. You generally will get a tax credit against either your U.S. taxes or your foreign income taxes, depending on your particular circumstances, so you will not be subject to double taxation.

If the country where you are living has an income tax treaty with the U.S., the treaty may contain so-called "tie-breaker rules" to determine which country will be treated as the country of your residence for income tax purposes. Usually, the location of the individual's permanent home or the center of the individual's vital interests determines resident status. If you are a resident of the treaty country under the tie-breaker rule and you elect to apply the treaty, you will be considered to be a resident of the treaty country for U.S. income tax purposes and will not be required to file a Form 1040. To make this election, you must file a U.S. Nonresident Alien Income Tax Return (Form 1040NR) in the year of the election and attach a copy of Form 8833 (Treaty-Based Return Position Disclosure under Section 6114 or 7701(b)). Green card holders who reside in a country that has an income tax treaty with the U.S. should contact an income tax professional or an office of the Internal Revenue Service for assistance.

What if I surrender my green card?
Generally, if you surrender your green card during the taxable year, your tax status as a resident alien will terminate on the last day of that calendar year. However, if you can establish that, for the remainder of the calendar year, your tax home is in a foreign country or you maintain a closer connection to that foreign country than to the United States, your residency termination date will be the date you surrender your green card.

If you are a resident of the United States because you meet both the substantial presence test for the taxable year and have a green card during the taxable year, your residency termination date will be the later of the date you surrender your green card or the last day you are physically present in the United States, provided you can establish one of the exceptions above. See Pub 519 (U.S. Tax Guide for Aliens) and the instructions to Form 8840 (Closer Connection Exception Statement for Aliens) for additional information. If you are a nonresident alien as of the last day of the year and a resident alien for a portion of the year, you should file a Form 1040NR even if you have no U.S. source income and attach a copy of Form 1040 that reflects your income for the period of the year that you were a resident alien.

What if I am a long-term resident when I surrender my green card?
If you are a long-term resident of the United States, defined as an individual who is a U.S. lawful permanent resident in at least 8 of the prior 15 taxable years prior to the termination of permanent resident status, there are special rules to comply with. Your residency termination date will not occur until you file a completed Form 8854 with the IRS and notify the Department of Homeland Security of your termination of residency, notwithstanding that for the remainder of the taxable year your tax home is in a foreign country or you have a closer connection to a foreign country. Until you file Form 8854 with the IRS and notify the Department of Homeland Security of your termination of residency, your termination of your permanent resident status for immigration purposes will not relieve you of your obligation to file U.S. tax returns and report your worldwide income as a resident of the United States. For purposes of U.S. tax rules, the date of your termination of residency will be the later of the date you notify the Department of Homeland Security or the date Form 8854 is filed with the IRS in accordance with the instructions for the form.

How do I give notice to the Department Of Homeland Security that I terminated my residency status?
You will be considered to have given notice of a termination of residency to the Secretary of Homeland Security as of the date that you complete Form I-407 (Abandonment of Lawful Permanent Resident Status) before a diplomatic or consular officer of the United States or at a Port of Entry of the United States before a U.S. immigration official.

What if I have had my green card for less than 8 years out of the last 15 taxable years at the time I revoke or abandon my green card?
You do not need to file a Form 8854 for any reason.

If I am a long-term resident, must I file Form 8854 for the next 10 years after I surrender my green card?
You must file a Form 8854 for each of the 10 tax years after the date of your abandonment of your long-term resident status only if:

(a) your average annual net income tax liability for the 5 years ending before the date of your termination of residency is more than a set amount ($124,000 for 2004, $127,000 for 2005, $131,000 for 2006),
(b) your net worth is $2 million or more on the date of your termination of residency, or
(c) you fail to certify on Form 8854 that you have complied with all of your U.S. federal tax obligations for the 5 years preceding the date of your termination of residency.

Failure to file a required Form 8854 in any of the 10 tax years after the date of your termination of residency may result in a $10,000 penalty for each year that the form is required but not filed.

Where do I get Form 8854?
The form is accessible on the internet at: http://www.irs.gov/formspubs/index.html

Taxation under section 877
If you are subject to section 877, you will be subject to an alternative tax regime with respect to your U.S. source gross income. For this limited purpose, special source and taxation rules apply; you should consider consulting a tax advisor as to the specific consequences. You generally will not be able to claim the benefits of an income tax treaty to reduce or exempt your income from U.S. taxation because the United States reserves the right to tax former citizens and long term residents according to U.S. law in almost all of its treaties. If you are subject to section 877 and you spend more than 30 days during any calendar year in the United States within the ten years following your termination of residency, you may be treated as a resident of the United States for tax purposes for that entire calendar year.

Expat Tax Obligations

U.S. Income Tax Obligation While Living Abroad
As a U.S. citizen/green card holder residing abroad, you still owe U.S. taxes each year on your worldwide income. The U.S. has tax treaties with many countries which allows the federal government to exchange data on its citizens living in other countries for tax purposes. Under some treaties, residents or citizens of the United States are taxed at a reduced rate, or are exempt from foreign taxes, on certain items of income they receive from foreign income.

Tax Position of U.S. Citizens Overseas
The IRS applies taxation rules on the basis of the taxpayer nationality and not on the basis of their residence. US expatriates who meet the Physical Presence Test or meet the Bona Fide Resident Test may be able to take advantage of the Foreign Earned Income Exclusion and or the Foreign Housing Exclusion.

You are considered physically present in a foreign country (or countries) if you reside in that country (or countries) for at least 330 full days in a 12-month period. You can live and work in any number of foreign countries, but you must be physically present in those countries for at least 330 full days. The qualifying period can be any consecutive 12-month period of time. A "full day" is 24 hours; days of arrival and departure are generally not counted in the physical presence test.

A person is considered a "bona fide resident" of a foreign country if they reside in that country for "an uninterrupted period that includes an entire tax year." A tax year is January 1 through December 31. Brief trips or vacations outside the foreign country will not jeopardize status as a bona fide resident. If the foreign government concerned has determined that a person is not subject to their tax laws as a resident, the Exclusions will not be available.

US citizens and resident aliens who are outside the United States (and its possessions) have the same requirements to file tax returns as anyone living in the United States. Income from worldwide sources must be considered when determining if a federal tax return must be filed. In general, foreign earned income is income received for services performed in a foreign country.

If you pay foreign taxes, it may be possible to offset these against US taxes if there is a double tax treaty with the country in which you are resident. The concept of 'tax home' is used in connection with foreign residence. Generally, a person tax home is the general area of their main place of business, employment, or post of duty where she is permanently or indefinitely engaged to work. A person is not considered to have a tax home in a foreign country for any period during which their abode (the place where they regularly live) is in the United States.

Foreign Earned Income Exclusion
If you are a full time resident abroad for a full calendar year, or live there for 330 days out of any consecutive 12-month period, you can exclude up to $95,100 (2012) of earned income from U.S. Income Taxation. If you are married, and both of you earn income and reside abroad, you can also exclude up to another $95,100 of your spouse's income from taxation. These exclusions can only be claimed by filing a tax return and are not automatic.

They cannot be claimed if you fail to file your Form 1040 for the applicable year (as well as the appropriate forms claiming this exclusion).

Earned income is income you earn for your work or services and does not include rental income, dividend or interest income, or other types of income that are not paid for your own personal efforts. You can also claim an additional exclusion or deduction for your foreign housing expenses exceeding a standard amount established by the Federal Government.

A person who claims the Exclusion cannot claim any credits or deductions that are related to the excluded income, for instance a foreign tax credit or deduction for any foreign income tax paid on the excluded income. The earned income credit is also unavailable furthermore, for IRA purposes, the excluded income is not considered compensation and, for figuring deductible contributions in an employer retirement plan, is included in modified adjusted gross income.

The IRS confirmed that: "Effective for tax years beginning after 2005, the amount of foreign earned income (and foreign housing costs) excluded from an individual gross income will be used for purposes of determining the rate of income and alternative minimum tax (AMT) that applies to his or her non-excluded income." The Tax Increase Prevention and Reconciliation Act of 2005 (P.L. 109-222) addded a new section 911(f) to the Internal Revenue Code. An individual tax will be the excess of the tax that would be imposed if his or her taxable income were increased by the amount(s) excluded, and the tax that would be imposed if his or her taxable income were equal to the excluded amount(s).

"For this purpose, the excluded amount(s) will be reduced by the aggregate amount of any deductions or other exclusions otherwise disallowed. In many cases this will have the effect of increasing an individual U.S. federal income tax to an amount greater than it would have been under prior law."

Beginning with tax year 2006, a qualifying individual claiming the foreign earned income exclusion, the housing exclusion, or both, had to calculate the tax on the remaining non-excluded income using the tax rates that would have applied had the individual not claimed the exclusions.

Generally, a qualifying individual initial choice of the foreign earned income exclusion must be made with one of the following income tax returns:

A return filed by the due date (including any extensions),

A return amending a timely-filed return. Amended returns generally must be filed by the later of 3 years after the filing date of the original return or 2 years after the tax is paid, or

A return filed within 1 year from the original due date of the return (determined without regard to any extensions).

Foreign Income Exclusion Is Not an Excuse for Non-Filing
It is a common mistake to believe you do not have to file a tax return if you make less than the foreign earned income exclusion. You can only take the exclusion by filing a return. If you are caught for not filing, you may not be allowed to use the exclusion.

Foreign Tax Credits

Foreign taxes paid by a US taxpayer can often be credited against US tax liability or deducted in figuring taxable income on a US income tax return. It is often better to claim a credit for foreign taxes rather than to deduct them. Whereas a credit reduces US tax liability, with any excess able to be carried back and carried forward to other years, a deduction reduces taxable income and may be taken only in the current year. All foreign income taxes must be given the same treatment; it isn't permitted to deduct some foreign income taxes and take a credit for others.

In order to take a foreign tax credit, Form 1116 should be filed with Form 1040. Form 1116 is used to figure the amount of foreign tax paid or accrued that can be claimed as a foreign tax credit. The foreign income tax on which a credit can be claimed is the amount of legal and actual tax liability paid or accrued during the year.

A foreign tax credit cannot be claimed in respect of tax that would be refunded by the foreign country if applied for, or if the foreign country returns tax payments in the form of a subsidy. Credits cannot be claimed in respect of foreign taxes paid on income that is excluded from a US tax return.

Foreign tax credits are limited to a proportion of total US tax liability equal to the proportion formed by taxable income from sources outside the United States of total taxable income. Foreign tax credits are figured separately in relation to different types of income, including: passive (investment) income; financial services income; shipping income; dividends from a domestic international sales corporation (DISC); lump-sum distributions from employer benefit plans; and section 901(j) income.

Expenses (such as itemized deductions or the standard deduction) not definitely related to specific items of income must be apportioned to the foreign income in each category in the proportions that the various types of income form of total income.

The foreign tax credit and deduction, their limits, and the carryback and carryover provisions are discussed in detail in IRS Publication 514, Foreign Tax Credit for Individuals. Taxes for Expats can help you claim Foreign Tax Credits that can be used to partially or completely offset U.S. taxes that accrue on this same income. In higher tax countries, you will accrue such tax credits faster than you will ever be able to apply them; in lower tax countries, you will likely be able to apply most or all such tax credits against U.S. tax liability on this same income.

U.S. Tax Treaties with over 60 Countries

The U.S. has Tax Treaties with over 60 other countries. A Tax Treaty is complex and includes many provisions that can benefit any U.S. taxpayer. Tax Treaties codify the objectives of reducing or eliminating double taxation of your income by both countries via reciprocal foreign tax credits (see previous section). Individual tax treaties also address tax issues specific to the two countries involved. If you file your tax return each year while living abroad, the statute of limitations for IRS audits will expire three years after you file those returns. That means the IRS cannot go back (unless there is evidence of fraud) and attempt to audit or change those returns later. You may want to consider filing your return even if you have no income or don't owe taxes in order to force the statute of limitations to run out, thereby eliminating any future problems when you decide to return to the U.S.

U.S. Social Security, Medicare, and Self-Employment Taxes

If you are an offshore employee of a U.S. corporation, that employer will normally withhold Social Security and Medicare taxes on your W-2 earnings. If you are working for a U.S.-based employer in one of the 20-plus countries with which the U.S. has established a Social Security Totalization Treaty, you may cite a closer connection to the foreign country and participate in that country social insurance system, and not have U.S. Social Security and Medicare taxes withheld from your U.S. pay.

If you are a bona fide employee of a foreign employer and are subject to foreign laws governing their social security tax, you are not required to pay U.S. Social Security tax. If you are self-employed (an independent contractor), you are obligated to pay, in addition to your income tax, a U.S. Self-Employment tax that is both employer and employee share of Social Security and Medicare taxes. You must file a Schedule C with your U.S. tax return and pay U.S. Self-Employment Tax on your net earnings by filing a Schedule S-E. The Self-Employment Tax rate is 15.3% of net Schedule C income before any foreign income exclusion and the taxable net self-employment rate is not reduced by the previously mentioned foreign tax credits. Net earnings are income after all legal business expenses are deducted and include the income earned both in a foreign country and in the United States.

Due Date of Tax Return

If you have your personal permanent residence abroad on April 15th of any year, you get an automatic extension to file your tax return for the previous calendar year until June 15th. If you need more time, you can file further extension requests which can extend the due date of your tax return until October 15th. If you owe taxes, and fail to pay the estimated taxes by April 15th, you will be subject to interest and penalties for that underpayment. However, those penalties are not as severe as those imposed for failing to file your tax return in a timely manner. It is therefore advisable to always file an extension if you are going to file your return later than April 15th, even if you do not have the money to pay your estimated taxes at the time.

Avoiding Penalty and Interest on Tax Due

Even if you file an extension to October 15th, instead of April 15th, to file your US Income Tax Return, be aware that interest and underpayment penalty are charged as of April 15th. Further, the IRS can assess underpayment penalty (and interest) if the tax due is paid by April 15th, but no (or insufficient) estimated tax payments or withholding were made prior to paying the balance due on April 15th. This is because tax law requires sufficient regular payment or withholding (or combination) to be done throughout the tax year in order to avoid ALL underpayment penalties.

Minimum Filing Requirements

Do I Need to File a Tax Return?
Factors such as age, disability, filing status and income will determine whether or not the US federal government requires you to file a tax return. The charts below will assist you in determining this. However, not being required to file may not actually be a good reason not to. Later in this article we will discuss the reasons to file a tax return even when it is not required.

Minimum Income Requirements Based on Age and Status
There is not a set minimum income for filing a return. The amount varies according to both filing status and age. The minimum taxable income level for each group is listed in the following chart. If your income falls below what is listed for your age group and marital status, you are not required to file a return.

Filing Status	Age	Minimum Income Requirement
Single	Under 65	$9,500
	65 or older	$10,950
Head of Household	Under 65	$12,200
	65 or older	$13,650
Married Filing Jointly	Under 65 (both spouses)	$19,000
	65 or older (one spouse)	$20,150
	65 or older (both spouses)	$21,300
Married Filing Separately	Any age	$3,700
Qualifying Widow(er) with Dependent Children	Under 65	$15,300
	65 or older	$16,450

Age and Status Requirements for Dependents
Being claimed as a dependent on someone else's taxes changes the rules a bit, and it does not rule out the possibility that you will still be required to file. If you are an adult, working dependent, it is very likely that you will be required to file your own return.

Marriage Status	Age	Minimum Income Requirement
Single	Under 65 (and not blind)	$5,800 earned (or $950 unearned)
	65 or older OR blind	$7,250 earned (or $2,400 unearned)
	65 or older AND blind	$8,700 earned (or $3,850 unearned)
Married	Under 65 (and not blind)	$5,800 earned (or $950 unearned)
	65 or older OR blind	$6,950 earned (or $2,100 unearned)
	65 or older AND blind	$8,100 earned (or $3,250 unearned)

Special Circumstances

Even if your income bracket is below the minimum listed for your age group and status, you usually must file a Federal Tax Return if you fall into any of the following "special circumstances" categories.

- If your self-employment earnings totaled $400 or more
- If you owe tax on a health savings account or a retirement plan
- If you owe Alternative Minimum Tax
- If you owe household employment taxes
- If you earned $108.28 + from a tax-exempt church or church-controlled organization
- If you received distributions from a Health Savings Account or an MSA
- If you are required to repay a 2008 Homebuyer Credit (or other recapture tax)
- If you owe Social Security/Medicare taxes on unreported income (tips)

Why You May Want to File Anyway

Not being required to file may be a bad reason not to do so, especially if you could use a little extra money following the holiday season. Refunds cannot be claimed without filing a return. Here are some reasons why a refund might be due to you:

- If you qualify for the First-Time Homebuyer Credit
- If you qualify for the Health Coverage Tax Credit
- If you have overpaid estimated tax
- If you qualify for a federal fuel tax credit
- If taxes were withheld from your pay
- If you qualify for the Earned Income Tax Credit
- If you qualify for the American Opportunity Credit
- If you have children and qualify for the Child Tax Credit
- If you adopted a child and qualify for the Adoption Tax Credit.
- If you can claim the Credit for Prior Year Minimum Tax

Earned vs. Unearned Income

In order to claim the foreign earned income exclusion (http://www.us-taxman.com/feie.php) you must have worked in a foreign territory when earning income. Any work performed in a foreign country is considered foreign income even if the payments are deposited into a US bank. Discerning between earned income and unearned income for the purposes of filing as an international employee can be difficult to say the least. To make things a bit less complicated, we will take a look at each aspect of foreign taxation and determine the appropriate income status of each by reviewing various sections of the US Tax Code.

In the Tax Guide for US, Publication 54, income is defined as compensation for professional services rendered. **Earned income on an international assignment may include any of the following types of compensation:**

- Bonuses
- Commissions
- Salaries
- Sick leave
- Severance pay
- Tips
- Vacation pay
- Wages
- Non-Cash income (meal & lodging reimbursements, use of company car, etc.)

Comparable in size to the list of earned income qualifiers, here is as impressive list for unearned income:

- Alimony
- Annuities
- Capital gains
- Corporate dividends
- Gambling earnings
- Interest
- Unemployment
- Social Security

Other Variable Income

Not every type of income is as black and white as the previous lists, however. There are numerous types of income which have very specific regulations which vary greatly depending on individual circumstances. For example, rental income is generally viewed as unearned income. In the case of an owner's or investor's direct involvement with the business of renting, however, a percentage of rental income not to exceed 30% can be viewed as earned income.

In the field of entertainment actors, actresses, dancers, singers and performers are usually paid directly for services performed or through royalty earnings based on distribution. A carpenter who renders payment for services will undoubtedly have received earned income. Writers and entertainers, however, will only have their royalties regarded as earned income in the event that there is a copyright transfer or a detailed contract was in place to submit a certain amount of literary works.

In regard to corporate income, Section 911(d)(2)(A) clearly defines the difference between earned income and unearned income - even in the event of salary compensation. This section of the United States Tax Code indicates that only reasonable compensation for services is considered earned income. If a CFO, for example, earned $140,000 in a year and the reasonable compensation rate was $85,000, then only $85,000 would be considered earned income. Industry averages for positions are used by the IRS to determine the rate of reasonable income.

While it's impossible to outline all of the variable businesses and types of income in each industry in one article, we can go over a few basic rules to help you determine whether your income is earned or unearned. In Section 911(d)(2)(B) earned income is defined as any income for which personal services were provided. It also states that any income derived from capital investments is generally considered unearned income; but if there is a net profit from capital investments and you performed work for the corporation through which investments were bought only 30% will be viewed as earned income.

We will provide an example of this situation. If you are a bona fide resident of Afghanistan earning $65,000 and you own a share of Deutsche Bank on the Borse which paid you roughly $25,000 your total earned income would equal the $65,000 you earned as salary. If, however, you performed services for Deutsche Bank your total earned income would equal $68,750 {($25,000x0.15) +$65,000}.

Split Year Income

There are cases in which foreign earned income is not earned until the following year. In this situation, according to Regulation Section 1.911-3(e)(1) all income earned in the first year must be filed with that year's taxes – regardless of the time in which compensation was realized. If you are performing services this year for which you do not anticipate receiving compensation until next year, remember that you must claim the foreign earned income on the current year's tax returns.

It's important to note, however that Code Section 911(b)(B) has different statutes for compensation received in the 3rd year after work was performed. In this case, the foreign earned income would be claimed in year 3, rather than in year 1.

What's equally as important to remember is that the previous 2 paragraphs are referring only to foreign earned income – not gross income. Gross income needs to be calculated in the year it was received, despite of the year in which it was earned. For example, if you work in 2012 but will not be paid for your services until 2013 you will not claim your earnings on your 2012 taxes; instead, you will claim them on your 2013 taxes when you file in 2014. If you will not be compensated until 2014 you will claim your income on your 2014 taxes you file in 2015.

As you have just learned, there are a great number of rules and regulations governing the definition of earned and unearned income. It is vital that you familiarize yourself with the specific rules in regard to your profession so that you can get the most out of the tax advantages offered to you as an international employee.

Foreign Income Exclusion

The Foreign Earned Income Exclusion

The Foreign Earned Income Exclusion is the largest tax advantage available to you as an expat. If elected, your first $95,100 earned overseas can be excluded from income tax, unless you are an employee of the US government. Note that if you are a Foreign Service employee, and your spouse works in the local economy, the exclusion still applies for your spouse. The following page is divided in two sections - a brief Executive Summary and Detailed Explanation of the Foreign Earned Income Exclusion.

Executive Summary of Foreign Earned Income Exclusion

The Residence Test

In order to benefit from the Foreign Earned Income Exclusion, the taxpayer must meet one of the following two criteria:

- Work full time inside a foreign country for an entire calendar year- known as the Bona Fide Residence Test
- Work outside of the United States for at least 330 of any 365 day period - known as the Physical Presence Test

While the two criteria may appear to be similar, they are actually quite different in terms of how they apply to your US expat taxes. US Expats automatically become eligible for the exclusion if they have worked overseas throughout an entire calendar year (January 1st- December 31st). They are then considered a bona fide resident. The second clause can be more confusing when applying to Expatriate tax return.

The second clause essentially means that a person left the United States for business and has not returned for more than 35 days throughout the past twelve months. This clause in not based on a calendar year; it simply refers to any twelve month period (i.e. April to April or September to September). Also note that it makes no reference to consecutive days; so a US Expat would be considered ineligible if he made several 2-7 day trips back to the US that totaled more than 35 days during the twelve month period in question. The key to meeting the "physical presence test" is to have spent less than 35 days in the US during a 12 month period.

The Deductions

If a person meets either of the above conditions they are allowed to deduct up to $95,100 of their foreign earned income from their US expat taxes. If you are married filing jointly, you would be able to deduct up to $190,200 from your US expat taxes for the 2012 tax year. This amount is also indexed for inflation and increases each year. Additionally, you would qualify for the Foreign Housing Deduction as well.

As the name implies, the Foreign Earned Income Exclusion relies solely on foreign income for calculation purposes and the income must be earned. Foreign income from sources such as dividends, interest and rental income are not included since this income is not "earned" in the IRS's view. Additionally, US based income from things such as pensions will not qualify for this exclusion because it was not earned inside a foreign country.

Common Pitfalls

There are some catches and loopholes to the Foreign Earned Income Exclusion, so it is almost always advisable to consult a US Expat tax expert about your specific situation. For example, business owners may be forced to pay the Self-Employment tax inside the US and this is not considered part of the Foreign Earned Income Exclusion. However you may still be able to exclude your earnings after you have paid the self-employment tax. Another common scenario for the self-employed is when US Expats move to countries where there is a Social Security treaty in place with the United States, like the UK. The US / UK treaty allows you to opt out of Social Security and enroll in the UK National Insurance Plan. By opting out of US social security, you could save about 15% annually on your US expat taxes!

The last thing worth mentioning is that not all US expats are able to take advantage of the foreign earned income exclusion. If you are a US Government Employee and are paid by the US government then you will not be able to use the Foreign Earned Income Exclusion to minimize your US expat taxes. This includes individuals in the Armed Forces Exchange, Commissioned and non-commissioned Officers' messes, Armed Forces motion pictures services and employees of kindergartens on Armed Forces installations.

Other considerations and opportunities that American expatriates should be aware of include the following:

- **Need to File State Returns**: Certain taxpayers must maintain a state of domicile in the United States, and there will be tax obligations to that state (Varies by state, please contact us for details).
- **Foreign Housing Exclusion or Deduction**: In addition to the foreign earned income exclusion, you can also claim an exclusion or a deduction from gross income for your housing amount if your tax home is in a foreign country, you have self-employment income, and you qualify under either the bona fide residence test or the physical presence test.
- **Retirement**: You still qualify for the tax advantages of making contributions to a retirement account, such as SEP, IRA or ROTH IRA. These contributions are subject to certain limits based on your gross income, so for the most part the foreign earned income exclusion will not affect them.
- **Other Income**: Did you rent your property while living abroad? Your rental income is reported, along with related expenses including but not limited to mortgage interest expense. Dividend or other investment income? Reported, less related expenses.
- **Are you self-employed but working overseas?** You are in need of a tax plan. You could be saving at least 6% of your gross income.

Detailed Explanation of Foreign Earned Income Exclusion

Following are **excerpts** from IRS Publication 54, Tax Guide for U.S. Citizens and Resident Aliens Abroad. Go here (http://www.taxesforexpats.com/pdf/p54.pdf) to download the complete publication [1.5 MB]. Below we present the key elements of qualifying for the Foreign Earned Income Exclusion, but you should consult the full publication for a complete explanation.

Who Qualifies for the Exclusions and the Deduction?

If you meet certain requirements, you may qualify for the foreign earned income and foreign housing exclusions and the foreign housing deduction.

If you are a U.S. citizen or a resident alien of the United States and you live abroad, you are taxed on your worldwide income. However, you may qualify to exclude from income up to $91,500 (for 2010) of your foreign earnings. In addition, you can exclude or deduct certain foreign housing amounts.

Requirements

To claim the foreign earned income exclusion, the foreign housing exclusion, or the foreign housing deduction, you must meet all three of the following requirements.

- Your tax home must be in a foreign country.
- You must have foreign earned income.
- You must be either:
- A U.S. citizen who is a bona fide resident of a foreign country of countries for an uninterrupted period that includes an entire tax year,
- A U.S. resident alien who is a citizen or national of a country with which the United States has an income tax treaty in effect and who is a bona fide resident of a foreign country or countries for an uninterrupted period that includes an entire tax year, or
- A U.S. citizen or a U.S. resident alien who is physically present in a foreign country or countries for at least 330 full days during any period of 12 consecutive months.

Tax Home in Foreign Country

To qualify for the foreign earned income exclusion, the foreign housing exclusion, or the foreign housing deduction, your tax home must be in a foreign country throughout your period of bona fide residence or physical presence abroad.

Tax Home

Your tax home is the general area of your main place of business, employment, or post of duty, regardless of where you maintain your family home. Your tax home is the place where you are permanently or indefinitely engaged to work as an employee of self-employed individual. Having a "tax home" in a given location does not necessarily mean that the given location in your residence or domicile for tax purposes.

Temporary or Indefinite Assignment

The location of your tax home often depends on whether your assignment is temporary or indefinite. If you are temporarily absent from your tax home in the United States on business, you may be able to deduct your away-from-home expenses (for travel, meals, and lodging), but you would not qualify for the foreign earned income exclusion. If your new work assignment is for an indefinite period, your new place of employment becomes your tax home and you would not be able to deduct any of the related expenses that you have in the general area of this new work assignment. If your new tax home is in a foreign country and you meet the other requirements, you earnings may qualify for the foreign earned income exclusion.

- If you expect your employment away from home in a single location to last, and it does last, for 1 year or less, it is temporary unless facts and circumstances indicate otherwise.
- If you expect it to last for more than 1 year, it is indefinite.

- If you expect it to last for 1 year or less, but at some later date you expect it to last longer than 1 year, it is temporary (in the absence of facts and circumstances indicating otherwise) until your expectation changes. Once your expectation changes, it is indefinite.

Bona Fide Residence Test

You meet the bona fide residence test if you are a bona fide resident of a foreign country or countries for an uninterrupted period that includes an entire tax year. You can use the bona fide residence test to qualify for the exclusions and the deduction only if you are either:

- A U.S. citizen, or
- A U.S. resident alien who is a citizen or national of a country with which the United States has an income tax treaty in effect.

You do not automatically acquire bona fide resident status merely by living in a foreign country or countries for 1 year. If you go to a foreign country to work on a particular job for a specified period of time, you ordinarily will not be regarded as a bona fide resident of that country even though you work there for 1 tax year or longer. The length of your stay and the nature of your job are only some of the factors to be considered in determining whether you meet the bona fide residence test.

Bona fide residence. To meet the bona fide residence test, you must have established a bona fide residence in a foreign country.

Your bona fide residence is not necessarily the same as your domicile. Your domicile is your permanent home, the place to which you always return or intend to return.

Example. You could have your domicile in Cleveland, Ohio and a bona fide residence in Edinburgh, Scotland, if you intend to return eventually to Cleveland.

The fact that you go to Scotland does not automatically make Scotland your bona fide residence. If you go there as a tourist, or on a short business trip, and return to the United States, you have not established bona fide residence in Scotland. But if you go to Scotland to work for an indefinite or extended period and you set up permanent quarters there for yourself and your family, you probably have established a bona fide residence in a foreign country, even though you intend to return eventually to the United States. You are clearly not a resident of Scotland in the first instance. However, in the second, you are a resident because your stay in Scotland appears to be permanent. If your residency is not as clearly defined as either of these illustrations, it may be more difficult to decide whether you have established a bona fide residence.

Determination. Questions of bona fide residence are determined according to each individual case, taking into account factors such as your intention, the purpose of your trip, and the nature and length of your stay abroad.

Statement to foreign authorities. You are not considered a bona fide resident of a foreign country if you make a statement to the authorities of that country that you are not a resident of that country, and the authorities:

- Hold that you are not subject to their income tax laws as a resident, or
- Have not made a final decision on your status.

Special agreements and treaties. An income tax exemption provided in a treaty or other international agreement will not in itself prevent you from being a bona fide resident of a foreign country. Whether a treaty prevents you from becoming a bona fide resident of a foreign country is determined under all provisions of the treaty, including specific provisions relating to residence or privileges and immunities.

Uninterrupted period including entire tax year - To meet the bona fide residence test, you must reside in a foreign country or countries for an uninterrupted period that includes an entire tax year. An entire tax year is from January 1 through December 31 for taxpayers who file their income tax returns on a calendar year basis.

During the period of bona fide residence in a foreign country, you can leave the country for brief or temporary trips back to the United States or elsewhere for vacation or business. To keep you status as a bona fide resident of a foreign country, you must have a clear intention of returning from such trips, without unreasonable delay, to your foreign residence or to a new bona fide residence in another foreign country.

Example 1. You arrived with your family in Lisbon, Portugal, on November 1, 2006. Your assignment is indefinite, and you intend to live there with your family until your company sends you to a new post. You immediately established residence there. You spent April of 2007 at a business conference in the United States. Your family stayed in Lisbon. Immediately following the conference, you returned to Lisbon and continued living there. On January 1, 2008, you completed an uninterrupted period of residence for a full tax year (2007), and you meet the bona fide residence test.

Example 2. Assume the same facts as in Example 1, except that you transferred back to the United States on December 13, 2007. You would not meet the bona fide residence test because your bona fide residence in the foreign country, although it lasted more than a year, did not include a full tax year. You may, however, qualify for the foreign earned income exclusion or the housing exclusion or deduction under the physical presence test (discussed later).

Bona fide resident for part of a year. Once you have established bona fide residence in a foreign country for an uninterrupted period that includes an entire tax year, you are a bona fide resident of that country for the period starting with the date you actually began the residence and ending with the date you abandon the foreign residence. Your period of bona fide residence can include an entire tax year plus parts of 2 other tax years.

Example. You were a bona fide resident of Singapore from March 1, 2006, through September 14, 2008. On September 15, 2008, you returned to the United States. Since you were a bona fide resident of a foreign country for all of 2007, you were also a bona fide resident of a foreign country from March 1, 2006, through the end of 2006 and from January 1, 2008 through September 14, 2008.

Reassignment. If you are assigned from one foreign post to another, you may or may not have a break in foreign residence between your assignments, depending on the circumstances.

Example 1. You were a resident of Pakistan from October 1, 2007, through November 30, 2008. On December 1, 2008, you and your family returned to the United States to wait for an assignment to another foreign country. Your household goods also were returned to the United States.

Your foreign residence ended on November 30, 2008, and did not begin again until after you were assigned to another foreign country and physically entered that country. Since you were not a bona fide resident of a foreign country for the entire tax year of 2007 or 2008, you do not meet the bona fide residence test in either year. You may, however, qualify for the foreign earned income exclusion or the housing exclusion or deduction under the physical presence test, discussed later.

Example 2. Assume the same facts as in *Example 1*, except that upon completion of your assignment in Pakistan you were given a new assignment to Turkey. On December 1, 2008, you and your family returned to the United States for a month's vacation. On January 2, 2009, you arrived in Turkey for your new assignment. Because you did not interrupt your bona fide residence abroad, you meet the bona fide residence test.

Physical Presence Test

You meet the physical presence test if you are physically present in a foreign country or countries 330 full days during a period of 12 consecutive months. The 330 days do not have to be consecutive. Any U.S. citizen or resident alien can use the physical presence to qualify for the exclusions and the deduction. The physical presence test is based only on how long you stay in a foreign country or countries. This test does not depend on the kind of residence you establish, your intentions about returning, or the nature and purpose of your stay abroad.

330 full days. Generally, to meet the physical presence test, you must be physically present in a foreign country or countries for at least 330 full days during a 12-month period. You can count days you spent abroad for any reason. You do not have to be in a foreign country only for employment purposes. You can be on vacation. You do not meet the physical presence test if illness, family problems, a vacation, or your employer's orders cause you to be present for less than the required amount of time.

Exception. You can be physically present in a foreign country or countries for less than 330 full days and still meet the physical presence test if you are required to leave a country because of war or civil unrest.

Full day. A full day is a period of 24 consecutive hours, beginning at midnight.

Travel. When you leave the United States to go directly to a foreign country or when you return directly to the United States from a foreign country, the time you spend on or over international waters does not count toward the 330-day total.

Example. You leave the United States for France by air on June 10. You arrive in France at 9:00 a.m. on June 11. Your first full day of physical presence in France is June 12.

Passing over a foreign country - If, in traveling from the United States to a foreign country, you pass over a foreign country before midnight of the day you leave, the first day you can count toward the 330-day total is the day following the day you leave the United States.

Example. You leave the United States by air at 9:30 a.m. on June 10 to travel to Kenya. You pass over western Africa at 11:00p.m. on June 10 and arrive in Kenya at 12:30 a.m. on June 11. Your first full day in a foreign country is June 11.

Change of location. You can move about from one place to another in a foreign country or to another foreign country without losing full days. If any part of your travel is not within any foreign country and takes less than 24 hours, you are considered to be in a foreign country during that part of travel.

Example 1. You leave Ireland by air at 11:00 p.m. on July 6 and arrive in Sweden at 5:00 a.m. on July 7. Your trip takes less than 24 hours and you lose no full days.

Example 2. You leave Norway by ship at 10:00 p.m. on July 6 and arrive in Portugal at 6:00 a.m. on July 8. Since your travel is not within a foreign country or countries and the trip takes more than 24 hours, you lose as full days July 6, 7, and 8. If you remain in Portugal, your next full day in a foreign country is July 9.

In United States while in transit. If you are in transit between two points outside the United States and are physically present in the United States for less than 24 hours, you are not treated as present in the United States during the transit. You are treated as traveling over areas not within any foreign country.

How to figure the 12-month period. There are four rules you should know when figuring the 12-month period.

- Your 12-month period can begin with any day of the month. It ends the day before the same calendar day, 12 months later.
- Your 12-month period must be made up of consecutive months. Any 12-month period can be used if the 330 days in a foreign country fall within that period.
- You do not have to begin your 12-month period with your first full day in a foreign country or end it with the day you leave. You can choose the 12-month period that gives you the greatest exclusion.
- In determining whether the 12-month period falls within a longer stay in the foreign country, 12-month periods can overlap one another.

Example 1. You are a construction worker who works on and off in a foreign country over a 20-month period. You might pick up the 330 full days in a 12-month period only during the middle months of the time you work in the foreign country because the first fiew and last few months of the 20-month period are broken up by long visits to the United States.

Example 2. You work in New Zealand for a 20-month period from January 1, 2007, though August 31, 2008, except that you spend 28 days in February 2007 and 28 days in February 2008 on vacation in the United States. You are present in New Zealand 330 full days during each of the following two 12-month periods: January 1, 2007 - December 31, 2007 and September 1, 2007 - August 31, 2008. By overlapping the 12-month periods in this way, you meet the physical presence test for the whole 20-month period.

Foreign Earned Income Exclusion

If your tax home is in a foreign country and you meet the bona fide residence test or the physical presence test, you can choose to exclude from your income a limited amount of your foreign earned income. You can also choose to exclude from your income a foreign housing amount.

If you choose to exclude foreign earned income, you cannot deduct, exclude, or claim a credit for any item that can be allocated to or charged against the excluded amounts. This includes any expenses, losses, or other normally deductible items allocable to the excluded income.

Limit on Excludable Amount

You may be able to exclude up to $95,100 of your foreign earned income in 2012. You cannot exclude more than the smaller of:

- $95,100, or

- Your foreign earned income for the tax year minus your foreign housing exclusion.

If both you and your spouse work abroad and each of you meet either the bona fide residence test or the physical presence test, you can each choose the foreign earned income exclusion. You do not both need to meet the same test. Together, you and your spouse can exclude as much as $190,200 for 2012.

Part-year exclusion. If the period for which you qualify for the foreign earned income exclusion includes only part of the year, you must adjust the maximum limit based on the number of qualifying days in the year. The number of qualifying days is the number of days in the year within the period on which you both:

- Have your tax home in a foreign country, and
- Meet either the bona fide residence test or the physical presence test.

For this purpose, you can count as qualifying days all days within a period of 12 consecutive months once you are physically present and have your tax home in a foreign country for 330 full days. To figure your maximum exclusion, multiply the maximum excludable amount for the year by the number of your qualifying days in the year, and then divide the result by the number of days in the year.

Foreign Housing Exclusion and Deduction

In addition to the foreign earned income exclusion, you can also claim an exclusion or a deduction from gross income for your housing amount if your tax home is in a foreign country and you qualify for the exclusions and deduction under either the bona fide residence test or the physical presence test.

The housing exclusion applies only to amounts considered paid for with employer-provided amounts. The housing deduction applies only to amounts paid for with self-employment earnings.

Foreign Housing Exclusion

The IRS does understand the predicament that is presented by moving and living overseas. The cost of living is simply not comparable. To not discourage Americans from moving overseas, the IRS allows expats to deduct certain housing expenses from their reported gross income. This deduction is referred to as the Foreign Housing Allowance (more specifically the Foreign Housing Exclusion or the Foreign Housing Deduction). This allowance will vary depending on your overseas location. In order to qualify for the allowance, you will need to spend enough time overseas to pass either the "bona fide resident" or "physical presence" test. Simply put, you need to actually live overseas to qualify. The Housing Exclusion applies to employed individuals (amounts paid by employers may be deducted), the Housing Deduction also applies to self-employed individuals.

How Much is Deductible?
Of course, there are limits as to how much and how many of your expenses you can deduct, and these limits are determined by the Foreign Earned Income Exclusion's limits (as a side note: you can claim the income exclusion, the housing exclusion, or both, but you can't exclude the same income for both). The 2012 FEIE is set at $95,100 (meaning that is the amount of foreign earned income that can be excluded from income reported to the IRS, if the FEIE is claimed). In regards to your housing deduction, you can normally expect to deduct no more than 30% of the FEIE limit. So, in 2012, one could deduct up to $28,530 (30% of $95,100). Things you can exclude until the deduction limit is reached are: necessary housing repairs, rent, water, gas, electricity, property insurance, parking and furniture/appliance rental. Things deemed lavish or unnecessary, such as pay television, will not qualify as deductions. Other things that do not qualify are taxes, domestic labor (maids, cooks, etc.), furniture purchases and property depreciation. Many expenses fall into an obvious category of need or want, but when the line is blurry, it is important to seek the advice of a professional.

Exceeding the Deduction Ceiling
In 2006, the Treasury and IRS began making adjustments for specific locations due to the extreme differentiation in the cost of living from that of the US. The IRS has since deemed over 400 locations to be exceptions to the 30% maximum deduction ceiling rule, and it has expanded the maximum limit for deductions for expats living within those locations. Examples of these higher allowances are London at $83,400; Singapore at $67,000; Bangkok $55,100; and Hong Kong at $114,300. Visit the IRS' list for details on all applicable locations.

Understanding Deduction Amounts According to Your Situation
Now that you're beginning to understand the housing allowance, you will want to delve into how much you, personally, will be able to deduct. First, you should consider how much you will not be able to deduct (the amount the IRS feels you would be paying if still in the US). This non-deductible amount is currently calculated as 16% of the FEIE, and this calculation is the same for everyone, regardless of location. With the FEIE at $95,100, the current amount that is required (completely non-deductible) is $15,216. It is important to calculate this amount in days ($41.69 per day), because days spent in the US will not count

toward your deductible amount. Now, if you live in Singapore, where the current allowance is $67,000 ($183.56 per day), and you spend 352 days outside of the US ($183.56 - $41.69) * 352, your deductible amount will be $49,938.24. Of course, knowing the exact amount you can deduct does not automatically tell you what to deduct. This can be a complicated process and should usually involve the help of a professional. In addition to the housing expenses mentioned above, employed individuals may also be able to deduct tax equalization and childcare/education expenses that are paid for by the employer.

Housing Deduction for the Self-Employed
Self-employed expats will not qualify for the foreign housing exclusion. But they can take advantage of the foreign housing deduction by deducting applicable housing expenses from their gross income. While the Foreign Housing Deduction will lower your overall tax liability, it will not reduce the Self-Employment Tax liability burden.

Housing Allowance or Income Exclusion?
As mentioned before, you cannot doubly claim income with the FEIE and the Housing Allowance. This is another issue that should be addressed with an international tax professional. Normally, it is wise to claim the housing allowance for income exceeding the FEIE limits.

How to Claim the Housing Allowance
Whether by way of the exclusion or the deduction, the Foreign Housing Allowance is a strictly voluntary matter. You will only be able to claim these allowances by filling out and including Form 2555 with your Federal Tax Return. The simplified Form 2555 EZ cannot be used for the housing exclusion or the deduction. The foreign housing deduction is reported on Form 2555 Part VI and IX. This deduction amount is then reported on Form 1040 Line 36, indicating "Form 2555" in the space provided.

Bonafide Residence Test

In order to qualify for certain deductions, expats must pass the Bona Fide Residence Test to determine whether they have truly set up residence in their overseas home. Your preparer will use this test to determine whether you are eligible for the Foreign Earned Income Exclusion. Living overseas does not necessarily mean that you qualify for expatriate status with the IRS. The requirements for every deduction and exclusion should be carefully reviewed, and expats should never simply assume that they qualify.

Bona Fide Resident Qualifications:
In order to claim the deductions and exclusions available to expatriates, you must meet each of these four requirements.

- You must be a US citizen (or resident alien living in a country that has a tax treaty with the US).
- You must have set up residence in a foreign country.
- You must live within that country for the whole year.
- You must not have any plans of moving away from your country of residence and returning to the US.

The requirements of the Bona Fide Resident Test are basically straightforward, except for the last point mentioned. Whether an expat has plans to return to the US can be difficult to determine. The following examples are intended to clarify this point.

Examples:

#1- An expatriate travels to Germany because of a two year work assignment. During the entire two years, he does not return home to the US. Even though he lives and works overseas for two years, he does not qualify for any exclusions or credits. He does not pass the Bona Fide Resident Test because he has predetermined to move back to the US.

#2- An expatriate buys a house in Ireland. Every year, he spends at least six months there with his family. He will never qualify as a Bona Fide Resident, however, because he still maintains residence in the US.

#3- An expatriate accepts a long term job in China. After the completion of his first year there, he would then qualify for credits and exclusions available to Bona Fide Residents. Although he may someday move back to the US, to qualify, he must have no immediate plans of doing so.

#4- An expatriate moves to India for work and he takes his family with him. After a few months, his company sends him back to the US for four weeks of job training. After a year, he will qualify as a Bona Fide Resident. He has truly set up residence in India and has no plans of moving back to the US. As a Bona Fide resident he will qualify for the Foreign Tax Credit, Foreign Housing Credit and the Foreign Earned Income Exclusion.

Conclusion:
Whether or not you qualify as a Bona Fide Resident will dramatically affect your taxes as a US expat. The credits and exclusions that coincide with this label can save you thousands of dollars. It's important, especially as an expat, to have an expert prepare your taxes as the Bona Fide Resident Test is not simply cut and dry. The IRS handles each of these cases as they come. If you've moved overseas and are not entirely sure when or if you will return to the US, you will most likely qualify as a Bona Fide Resident after your first full year

abroad. To be sure, though, and to be sure that the relevant form (2555) has been completed correctly, it is wise to seek the assistance of an international tax expert.

Bonafide Residence Precautions

Most American expatriates are familiar with the term - Bona Fide Residency (http://www.us-taxman.com/bonified-r.php). Many even know that the Bona Fide Residency test is preferred over the Physical Presence Test. Why? Bona Fide Residency gives the expat the luxury of spending a month-long vacation in California, Thanksgiving week at the parents' house in Jersey, and the winter holiday season in Vermont without having to worry about the dreadful 330 days count. (Provided one has resources and desire to fly in and out of the United States).

Very few, however, understand who can qualify as a Bona Fide Resident in the foreign country and who cannot. In our practice we often encounter expats who made the mistake of using BFR status which was later disallowed by the IRS. The purpose of this article is to explain in **simple** terms when one can claim this status and how to not get caught off-guard by the IRS by doing it improperly. Lastly we will explain the consequences of claiming the status and having it later rejected by the IRS and how we can help you.

First let's start at the source. The IRS Publication 54 (http://www.irs.gov/pub/irs-pdf/p54.pdf) reads:

Questions of bona fide residence are determined according to each individual case, taking into account such factors as your intention or the purpose of your trip and the nature and length of your stay abroad.

Determined according to each individual case, ha! Not the most reassuring of definitions. Further reading reveals: *"To qualify for bona fide residence, you must reside in a foreign country for an uninterrupted period that includes an entire tax year. An entire tax year is from January 1 through December 31 for taxpayers who file their income tax returns on a calendar year basis."*

Well, what if you spent the entire year in Timbuktu and the following year you want to claim a Bona Fide Residency qualification? Here goes the next paragraph:

"You do not automatically acquire bona fide resident status merely by living in a foreign country or countries for 1 year."

Some expats, confused by these instructions, decide to double-proof their qualification for the foreign earned income exclusion and fill out both sections on form 2555EZ; Bona Fide Residency Test and Physical Presence Test. Usually it happens to those who think their taxes are so simple, the 2555EZ form will intuitively guide them through. The results are devastating.

Irrespective of the fact that the taxpayer could have qualified for the foreign earned income exclusion through one of the tests, **the IRS automatically rejects foreign income exclusion when both sections are filled**. The term "rejects" does not mean that the IRS sends you a note notifying you of your mistake and to kindly resend the amended form. Instead, the IRS accepts your tax return as is, yet treats the excluded income as taxable. Since examination usually occurs 18 to 24 months after filing, the IRS adds the interest accumulated over time and to "sweeten the deal", "Accuracy-related" penalties.

Hence, what are the criteria the IRS takes into account to make the determination on each individual case?

- First and foremost, residing in a foreign country for the entire calendar year and spending no more than 35 days (the fewer, the better) in the Unites States over that first year.
- The second criterion is the correct answer to the question on line 13a of form 2555, *"Have you submitted a statement to the authorities of the foreign country where you claim bona fide residence that you are not a resident of that country?"* The answer should always be **No**. Question 13b, *"Are you required to pay income tax to the country where you claim bona fide residence?"* is ambiguous. Generally, it is better to answer "Yes". What if you live in a tax heaven country without income tax? Answering "Yes" would be a lie. Then, answer "No". If other conditions for the Bona Fide residency are met, you will not become disqualified by the negative answer to this question.
- The third and very important criterion is the nature and length of your job. **If your work is contract-based with the established length of the contract, you may not qualify.** I say "May not" instead of "Do not" because there are other factors explained below that will be taken into consideration. Yet, generally speaking, a job with a finite employment length does not qualify an expat for the Bona Fide Residency status. Please note - this definitely applies to the government civilian contractors working in Conflict Zones. No matter how long you stay in Iraq, no matter how good employee you are that your contract will certainly be renewed, there is no way American citizen can claim himself Bona Fide Resident of Iraq (or Afghanistan, or Kuwait).
- Next thing the IRS will take into consideration is your housing status. If you purchased a house - great, your chances to qualify as a Bona Fide resident are very high. If you rent an apartment - acceptable but you must give more proof for qualification. Hotel is the least acceptable yet possible if other conditions are met. If you have free housing in an employer-provided barracks, then you are not a Bona Fide resident in the foreign country (another reason why civilian contractors in Conflict Zones do not qualify).
- Type of visa: If you have a student visa or a temporary work visa, the renewal of which is contingent upon your employment - you are not a Bona Fide resident. If you are a permanent resident or have a dual citizenship, then other factors have little bearing and you qualify as a Bona Fide Resident.
- Family composition: Family is important in general. For the purpose of our discussion, it is particularly important as a demonstration of your serious intent with regard to the stay in the foreign country. There is a reason why form 2555 asks you about people residing with you and the length of their stay. If you took along your wife and have two kids attending the local school, then the odds of being approved as a Bona Fide resident are very high. You can become unemployed but your family is with you, and you do not lose the Bona fide residency qualification.
- There is one factor conveniently disguised on form 2555, yet very important for the IRS determination of the Bona Fide Residency: if you get married to a citizen of the foreign country or have a common-law partner (domestic partner) citizen of that country, this alone increases your chances to become approved as a Bona Fide

resident. **You can add this detail on line 12a of form 2555 answering to the question who lives with you in the foreign country.**

- Questions 15d and 15e on form 2555, "Do you maintain a home in the United States while living abroad?" Not that there is anything wrong with maintaining a home in the Unites States - you can rent it out or let your second cousin live there free. However, if the answer to the question 15e "The name of the occupants and their relationship to you" reveals that your spouse and children live in that home of yours, then you are most probably not a Bona Fide resident and your intent is to complete the foreign job assignment and come back home to your beloved family.

Now - here comes the scary part. What exactly will happen when the IRS examines your return (this normally happens occurs 18 to 24 months after filing) and decides to disallow your Bona Fide status? Bear in mind - IRS has full discretion whether to allow or disallow it. So unless you can safely prove the criteria outlined above, it will likely be disallowed, with little recourse available to you.

In that case the IRS will simply take away the Foreign Earned Income Exclusion and slap penalties & interest on top. In dollar terms - assuming your income was $100,000 and you used up the entire FEIE (assume $90,000). If 2 years later the IRS comes knocking, the amount they would seek would be $50,000 (comprised of $25,000 in tax and $25,000 in interest and penalties). At this point you may want to ask yourself the Dirty Harry question - do you feel lucky enough to risk this?

Now, we don't want to end this on a sad note, so here is the good news. At Taxes for Expats we know exactly how to prepare expatriate tax returns and what other venues (i.e. ones that aren't as risky) are available to minimize your US tax liability. We have over 20 years of experience doing this. So talk to us first - we are here to help.

Physical Presence

Both the Bona Fide Resident Test and the Physical Presence Test apply to American expats. The Bona Fide Resident Test applies to those expats who live overseas and have no plans of returning to the US. To pass the Physical Presence Test, though, one must simply be away from the US for more than 329 out of 365 days. It is important to keep this test and its qualifications in mind when traveling to and from the US. Passing this tax test will greatly reduce, maybe even eliminate, your US taxes.

To pass the Physical Presence Test, your situation must reflect all of the following:
- You must be a US citizen or a resident alien
- You must be outside of the US and its territories for at least 330 days out of a consecutive 365.
- You must be legally inside your foreign country of residence.

Things to Consider:
Keep in mind that each day spent on US soil is counted against you. Even if you simply fly in for an afternoon meeting, the entire day will be deducted. There are significant tax credits and exclusions available to those who can prove physical presence in a foreign country (including the Foreign Housing Credit, the Foreign Earned Income Exclusion, and the Foreign Tax Credit). Therefore, whenever possible, it behooves expats to remain in the US for less than thirty five of every 365 days.

The Physical Presence Test applies to any 365 day time line. It can be counted from any day of any month. The test is very cut and dry and there are no exceptions counted for emergency travel. Any time spent on US soil counts against the necessary 330 days. Additionally, travel days (when traveling to the US) also count against the 330 days. Even if you pass the physical presence test and qualify for the exclusions, you might still be presented with a tax bill by the IRS. This is due to the fact that the exclusion only applies to money earned on foreign soil.

Examples:
#1- If an American expatriate opens a business in Tokyo, Japan on March 14th 2010 and then stays in Tokyo until February 23rd, he will automatically qualify for the Foreign Earned Income Exclusion. He has successfully passed the Physical Presence Test because he remained in Tokyo for 344 days.
#2- If the above expat traveled during those 344 days, but he did not travel to the US or its territories, he would still pass the Physical Presence Test and qualify for the expat exclusions.
#3- If the same business owner traveled back to the US for business reasons (or for any other reason) and spent more than fourteen days traveling to the US and on US soil, he would lower his time away below 330 days and no longer qualify for expat exclusions and credits.

Conclusion:
If your goal is to occupy two homes, one on US soil and one abroad, it will not be beneficial for you to try and claim expat exemptions. If, however, your intention is to primarily

occupy your foreign residence and spend very little time on US soil, you should plan your time in the US very carefully. If you can easily lower your time in the US to less than 330 days, the effort will probably be well worth it (depending on your taxable income). Consult an international tax expert to be sure you will qualify for the exclusions and credits available to you.

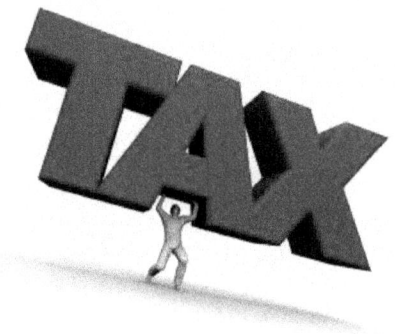

Foreign Spouse

If you are married to a non-American and you both live overseas, you may have wondered how this impacts on your U.S. tax filing situation, if at all. As with most concerns involving taxes, the more complicated they can make it, the better Congress likes it! This article will try to present your various tax obligations (and options) with regard to a non-American spouse as simply and precisely as possible.

The decision on how to treat your foreign spouse for income tax purposes is a critical part of Tax Planning. These are important points to consider:

If you intend to have your foreign spouse apply for a green card and eventually for the U.S. citizenship, it is in your best interest to treat him as a U.S. resident and file jointly.

If your spouse has a self-employment income you may choose to treat him as a nonresident and file separately. Then, his income is not a subject to U.S. income tax and self-employment tax.

If your non-resident spouse has foreign income from assets (e.g., rental income, capital gains, etc.) and you file as married filing separately or as head of household, this income is not a subject to U.S. income tax. If you file jointly, you must report this income on U.S. tax return.

Possibility #1 -- Spouse has "green card" or is otherwise considered "resident alien" If your spouse has obtained a green card, is a naturalized U.S. citizen or is otherwise considered a resident alien, the situation is relatively simple. Even if you both live overseas, as long as your spouse has the status of a resident alien, he/she will be taxed as if he/she was a U.S. citizen. This means world-wide income is taxed for both of you. Not only is the earned income of each spouse subject to U.S. taxation, but any investment income, even if earned in a foreign country with the foreign spouse as the sole recipient, is subject to U.S. tax. The good news is that you can use the filing status of "married, joint" so that you get a higher standard deduction and a personal exemption for each of you. Also, if you each qualify for the foreign earned income exclusion, you can exclude up to $91,500 (for 2010) per person per year of foreign income.

Note: If your spouse is a citizen of another country (while also a resident alien in the U.S.), and you happen to live in that country, special rules may apply. In the event the U.S. has a tax treaty with that country, you should take a look at the treaty and/or consult a tax professional in that country.

Possibility #2 -- Spouse is considered "nonresident alien (NRA)" for U.S. tax purposes. If your spouse has neither a green card nor resident alien status, he/she will be classified as a nonresident alien (NRA). If this is the case, you have 2 choices, each of which comes with its own set of complexities:

Should you choose to treat spouse as resident alien for tax purposes: If you follow this route, you must understand that you will have to report your spouse's worldwide income (as described above) and it will be subject to U.S. tax. You also should realize this is an active choice you make and there are certain procedures that must be followed to make it effective:

First, you have to attach a statement, signed by both spouses, to your tax return for the first year to which the choice applies. The statement must include a declaration that one spouse is a nonresident alien and the other is a U.S. citizen or resident alien, and you are choosing to both be treated as U.S. residents for the tax year. You also have to include the name, address and Social Security number (or Individual Taxpayer Identification number) of each spouse.

Second, note that for the first year you make the choice, you have to file a joint return. But in later years you can file joint or separate returns. It is also important to realize you must continue to file this way (treating both as U.S. citizens or resident aliens) unless you (or circumstances) end the choice. This can happen if either spouse revokes the choice in writing, either spouse dies, you have a legal separation or divorce, or the IRS ends the choice because it feels you haven't kept adequate records.

Example:

Anna Scott has been a US citizen for many years. She is married to Nikos, a nonresident alien. Joe and Nikos make the choice to treat Nikos as a resident alien by attaching a statement to their joint return. Anna and Nikos must report their worldwide income for the year they make the choice and for all later years unless the choice is ended or suspended. Although Anna and Nikos must file a joint return for the year they make the choice, they can file either joint or separate returns for later years.

You might wonder why you would go to all this trouble, especially if you have to declare the foreign spouse's income. The main reason is you will use the "married, joint" filing status which gives you a higher standard deduction and many other benefits that are not available if you use the "married, separate" filing status. Also, if your spouse does not work or his/her income is excluded as foreign income, you have no additional income on which you owe tax while still getting the benefits of the "married, joint" filing status.

Social Security Number

If your spouse is a nonresident alien and you file a joint or separate return, your spouse must have either a Social Security Number (SSN) or an Individual Taxpayer Identification Number (ITIN). We can help our clients obtain ITIN number for their nonresident spouses while they are living abroad. You would have to provide original or certified copies of documents to verify your spouse's age, identity, and citizenship.

Should you choose to treat spouse as nonresident alien for tax purposes: If you decide you don't want to include your NRA spouse's income on your U.S. tax return, you generally will have to use the filing status of "married, separate". However, if your spouse has no income from sources within the U.S. and is not claimed as a dependent of another U.S. taxpayer, you can claim an exemption for your NRA spouse. You need to be sure to obtain an Individual Taxpayer Identification number for your spouse before filing the return (We can help you obtain ITIN with the IRS). Furthermore, if you have other qualifying relatives living with you and you meet the other eligibility tests; you can file as "head of household". The tax rates and standard deduction for this filing status are much superior to that of the "married, separate" filing status.

Unlike the "choice" you made with regard to treating your spouse as a resident alien, there is no additional paperwork involved with treating your spouse as a nonresident alien for tax purposes. And if you find that the "married, separate" status has too many negative tax implications, you may decide that in future years you want to file "married, joint" by simply making the choice and attaching the statement described above.

ITIN New Rules

ITIN: Individual Tax Identification Number

An ITIN is an Individual Tax Identification Number issued by the IRS to certain taxpayers who – for one reason or another – are not eligible to have a Social Security Number issued to them. Some of these individuals include foreign exchange students, nonresident aliens, foreign nationals, and a variety of international or domestic individuals who are required by unique circumstances to pay US taxes or file an annual US tax return.

If you do not have a Social Security Number, are required to pay US taxes or file a US tax return, and you need to have an ITIN issued to you, you may request the issuance of an ITIN by completing Form W-7 and submitting it to the IRS. Make sure to pay close attention to this form, as there are items which require additional documentation to be submitted.

Beginning in June, 2012, the IRS ceased to accept copies of documentation submitted with Form W-7. As such, it's imperative that only original documents are submitted. If you have a certified copy from the agency which originally issued your documentation, this hard copy version is acceptable by IRS standards. For now, this is an interim ruling during the developmental phase of new ITIN application procedures, and there are only 2 groups who are not affected by this interim ruling: Spouses of military personnel or military personnel dependents without a valid Social Security Number (these individuals must check box e on Form W-7) and nonresident aliens who need an ITIN to take advantage of tax treaty benefits (these individuals must check box a and specify the reason for the request using box h on Form W-7).

On October 2, 2012, the IRS launched a new electronic application procedure for international students living in the United States through the SEVP (Student Exchange Visitors Program). This streamlined procedure can also be utilized by US expat taxpayers who have been approved for a filing extension from Tax Year 2011. The IRS has announced that the current system available online is a temporary measure until a final and even more streamlined system is available. The IRS expects the final streamlined application procedure to be available by January 1, 2013.

Required Documentation

As indicated earlier, when submitting Form W-7, additional documentation is required. The documents which are accepted by the IRS as valid forms of identification are:

- Birth certificate (ITIN applicants under the age of 18 are required to send)
- Foreign ID
- Foreign voter's registration card
- Medical records (for dependents of applicants only – under the age of 14, under 18 for students)
- National ID (must contain current photo and address, name, date of birth, and a future expiration date)
- Passport (does not require additional documentation)
- Travel or work Visa
- US state ID

- US Military ID
- USCIS (U.S. Citizenship and Immigration Services) photo ID
- Valid U.S. driver's license
- Valid foreign driver's license
- School records (for dependents of applicants only under the age of 14, under 18 for students)

In addition to being current (containing a future expiration date), all documentation must have a valid name and photograph and show proof of your foreign status. For documents on which expiration dates are not issued, the issue date must be within a timeframe of 12 months or less prior to the date submitted with an ITIN application.

The 2013 Year Update from the IRS
On Nov. 29, 2012 the Internal Revenue Service finalized the interim procedures to strengthen the Individual Taxpayer Identification Number (ITIN) program requirements http://www.irs.gov/uac/Newsroom/Updated-ITIN-Procedure-Changes-Announced

A key change is that, for the first time, new ITINs will expire after five years. This change will help ensure ITINs are being used for legitimate tax purposes. Taxpayers who still need an ITIN will be able to reapply at the end of the expiration period.

The finalized procedures are effective Jan. 1, 2013 in time for the 2013 tax-filing season when many ITIN applications are submitted along with a taxpayer's income tax return.

Double Taxation

Many U.S. taxpayers working overseas express concern about the risk of double taxation. Tax treaties existing between the U.S. and most foreign countries provide a specific mechanism for eliminating double taxation. This mechanism grants a credit for the taxes paid in the foreign country to reduce the taxes of a resident of the country. A limited amount of the foreign income tax you pay can be credited against your U.S. tax liability. Depending on the specific situation, using a full amount available foreign tax credit may be more beneficial to the expat than using foreign income exclusion. We analyze all options and offer the best tax-saving solution for each individual client.

List of Tax Treaties
A full list of countries which have tax treaties with the United States, and the agreements themselves, can be accessed via the Internal Revenue Service website (http://www.irs.gov/businesses/international/article/0,,id=96739,00.html) together with technical explanations in most cases. An updated treaty has recently been negotiated with the United Kingdom.

Foreign Tax Credit

Expats who live and work abroad are used to the problem of double taxation. This is due to the fact that U.S. citizens (and Green Card holders) are required to report their foreign income to the IRS as well as pay taxes to their country of residence.

There are two very useful aids for avoiding the problem of double taxation: the Foreign Earned Income Exclusion (http://www.us-taxman.com/feie.php) and **the Foreign Tax Credit**. These methods are both valuable, but under different circumstances. When faced with the choice - it is often more beneficial to use the Foreign Tax Credit alone; this article will explain the basics of this principle.

The Foreign Earned Income Exclusion (FEIE), Is It Beneficial?

In days gone by, the Foreign Earned Income Exclusion was every expat's method for avoiding double taxation. Especially since it was almost double the current amount in inflation adjusted terms (see graph). However, in 2006, President Bush signed the Tax Reconciliation Act of 2005. This eliminated the option of taking the massive deductions allowed by the FEIE ahead of other deductions and exemptions. The previous way of doing things had been hugely beneficial to high earning expats because it placed them in a lower tax bracket than they actually earned. Post 2006, it is often more advantageous to skip the FEIE and go strictly with the Foreign Tax Credit method of saving, however.

To be beneficial, the FEIE should only be used by Americans living in countries with either no income tax or an income tax rate that is lower than the American rate. You can check this page of our site (http://www.us-taxman.com/bracket.phpl) for what your US Federal income tax bracket is. If an expat resides in a country with a tax rate that is the same or higher than the American rate, disadvantages follow use of the Foreign Earned Income Exclusion.

MAGI

There is an important term that every expat must become familiar with. That term is Modified Adjusted Gross Income. This term becomes important for expats who are using or considering using the FEIE. With the exclusion, expats must add the excluded amount back into their adjusted gross income (AGI), making it a modified AGI.

Roth IRA and the Child Tax Credit

A ROTH IRA is a very valuable savings tool. One is allowed to contribute after tax dollars from taxable compensation in the amount of $5,000 ($6,000 for those who are 50 or over). Money deposited into a ROTH IRA can be invested freely or left alone to accrue interest that is completely tax free. However, if an expat has used the FEIE and has therefore excluded all of his income, he will have no taxable compensation to contribute to a ROTH IRA. Be warned! The Child Tax Credit is a valuable tax savings tool for parents as it credits a taxpayer $1,000 per minor child if the taxpayer earns under a specified amount. In fact, it is possible to receive this credit as a refund even when the expat owes no tax, as long as the taxpayer can prove taxable earned income. If all of expats earnings were excluded under the FEIE, he will lose the credit at $1,000 per child. Excluding all earned income, which is common under the FEIE, will result in an inability to qualify for benefits like a ROTH IRA or the Child Tax Credit because these tools require reportable earned income. If an expat chooses to save via the Foreign Tax Credit, however, he will still report taxable earned income and will qualify for the aforementioned savings tools. If an expats falls prey to the glimmering appeal of the FEIE, and then realizes after the fact that it was not beneficial under his circumstances, he will be allowed to retrace his taxes back to 2008 and file an amended return. Sadly, though, missed ROTH opportunities are gone forever.

The Exclusion and Foreign Tax Credit in Tandem

It is possible to use both the FEIE and the FTC in the same year. But using both while in a country whose tax rate is higher than that of the US is a waste of time and energy. It is absolutely possible to pay higher taxes by using the FEIE followed by the FTC than it would have been to use the FTC alone. The details are complex, however, and are the reason that international tax professionals are an invaluable resource for expats. When in doubt and with foreign taxes there is almost always reason to doubt, contact a tax professional (http://www.us-taxman.com/contact.php).

The Foreign Tax Credit (FTC)

The Foreign Tax Credit is useful for any American who has paid taxes overseas. The FTC does not obligate a person to prove residence in an overseas location. If a U.S. citizen works overseas or is involved in foreign investments, it is likely that he has paid taxes to a foreign government. If the tax rate of the foreign country is equal to or greater than the U.S. tax rate, the Foreign Tax Credit will successfully rid the expat of any U.S. tax obligation on that amount.

Simply put, by claiming the FTC the U.S. tax obligation is lowered by the amount paid to the foreign government. The qualifications are straightforward:

- Only income tax is credited.
- The credited amount cannot exceed the amount that would have been owed to the U.S. government. If the income tax paid to a foreign government far exceeds the amount of the credit (because the foreign tax rate far exceeded the US rate), the expat will forfeit that amount. The credit, however, can be carried into the future.
- Although they are foreign taxes, expats cannot claim a credit for taxes on:
- Excluded income (the Foreign Earned Income Exclusion, income from Puerto Rico and Possessions)
- Taxes Imposed By Sanctioned Countries (Cuba, Iran, Libya, North Korea, Sudan, Syria)
- Foreign mineral income
- International boycott operations
- U.S. persons controlling foreign corporations and partnerships who fail to file required information returns
- Foreign oil/gas extraction income

Foreign taxes that cannot be credited through Foreign Tax Credit method are still eligible to be claimed as part of itemized deductions.

Conclusion

Expats should never assume that something that applies to them is in their best interest. A tax break that is advantageous to one expat may be detrimental to another. Case in point: many unstudied applications of the FEIE over the FTC. Allow your money and the special expat credits to work for you by seeking the expert advice of a studied international tax professional.

FAQ

I have not filed for more than 5 years. What are my options now?
1. The best thing to do now is file your income taxes now and pay any related penalties and interest. Although you have to file only for those years where your earned income was more than a specified amount for that year or $400 if you are self-employed, we recommend filing for all past years to establish a 3-year statute of limitation break on your filing history.

I did not Know that I Had to Report my Global Income on my tax return. Now What?
2. You will need to submit the amended tax returns including all of your income. The best thing to do is to gather together your tax documents and your old returns and send them to us. We will file the amended return including your global income.

If I file for the previous years, do I lose my right to the foreign earned income exclusion?
3. If you are filing voluntary, you do not lose the right to the exclusion. I you are being audited, you lose this right.

Then, I would have no taxes due because of the foreign earned income exclusion, so why do I have to file?
4. You must file even if your tax due is zero.

I am self-employed; do I qualify for the foreign earned income exclusion?
5. Only for federal income taxes - but you are responsible for Medicare and social security taxes (and entitled to such benefits upon required age).

I own my own business overseas, which is a legal entity in my country of residence. Do I qualify for the foreign earned income exclusion, and do I have to pay social security and Medicare taxes?
6. You qualify for the exclusion from the income tax on compensation for personal services provided to your business. You do not have to pay U.S. Self-Employment tax on that income because this income is treated as wages, not as income from self-employment. You have, however, to file U.S. information return on the corporation or partnership you own in the foreign country..

I am a Foreign Service government employee; do I have to pay state taxes while living overseas?
7. Depending on your state of residence, you may or may not. Unfortunately the list is extensive - but if you contact us (http://www.us-taxman.com/contact.php) we would be happy to check.

I am a civilian working overseas in direct support of the US armed forces; do I qualify for combat pay income exclusion or any kind of extension of deadlines?
8. While you do not qualify for the combat zone military pay exclusion, as this exclusion only applies to members of the US Armed Forces, you do qualify for an extension for

the filing and paying of your income taxes. This extension gives you 180 days after your last day in the combat zone. During this period, no interest or penalties attributable to the extension period will be assessed.

Due to a medical emergency, I had to come to the US and because of this time I do not meet the 30 days for the physical presence test. is there an exception under medical emergencies?

9. No. The only exception for the 330 day requirement in the physical presence test is when you must leave the foreign country due to war or civil unrest.

Am I taxed on the market value of the residence that my employer provides for me while overseas?

10. Unless living in those quarters is mandated by your employer for business reasons, it is indeed taxable income (Though it could be part of your foreign earned income exclusion).

I have to pay US taxes, but I do not have US Dollars and my home country currency is not fully convertible. How can I comply with my duty to pay taxes?

11. If you face the issue of blocked income due to foreign currency restrictions in your home country, you could postpone the reporting and payment until the currency becomes unblocked, or pay with funds you may have in the US. If you decide to postpone you would file certain information and no penalties or interest would accrue.

I am a US Citizen and have not lived in the US since 2000. I maintain a residence visa in a foreign country and live there when I am not working. When I am working I work on a Cruise Ship; the ship is not registered in the USA. Do I qualify for the Foreign Earned Income Exclusion?

12. Yes, you do.

I inherited some money, does the foreign earned income exclusion apply?

13. No. The exclusion only applies to earned income (i.e. wages).

I was only a couple of days short of meeting the 330 days for the physical presence test! What luck! Is there anything I can do to avoid this large tax bill?

14. We can file an extension on your behalf, and wait to file until you have met the 330 day requirement (Yes, even if you are using days from the next fiscal year).

What is one of the most popular mistakes by taxpayers living abroad?

15. Not reporting your bank accounts abroad. This applies to any person that has a financial interest in, signature authority or other authority over any financial account(s) in a foreign country and the aggregate value of these account(s) exceeds $10,000 at any time during the calendar year. Not reporting can make you subject to civil and criminal penalties, and penalties of up to $100,000.

I am a US citizen and I have been working in Argentina for more than 5 years as a chemical engineer. I was not planning on staying this long in a foreign country but I have gotten married here and I plan to live here for many more years. Since I am not in the US, does that make paying federal taxes voluntary?

16. You are not exempt from paying taxes. You are taxed on the basis of your citizenship and not your residency. Americans are taxed differently from citizens in most countries. However, there are special exemptions that you may look into. There are credits for taxes that you pay to the country where you reside as well as the foreign earned income exclusion. Take note that this exclusion is adjusted for inflation annually and is estimated to be $95,100 in 2012. In addition, there is no statute of limitations on tax collections if you have never filed your income tax return. Obligations grow each year that they are not paid. To report income, you have to first file the right IRS form and the Form 2555 (Foreign Earned Income Form) or Form 2555-EZ, in addition to the IRS Form 1040. Form 2555 is for those who own houses and/or are self-employed. Form 2555-EZ is for those whose income is less than the amount of foreign income exclusions and will not be applying for housing and self-employment deductions. There still is an April 15th deadline but the IRS allows an automatic two-month extension to file the forms.

I started my job in Poland as an interior designer in July 2008 and went back to New Jersey in December 2008 to sell my car and my house there. It took me awhile and I resumed my job in Warsaw in July 2009. Am I entitled to the foreign earned income exclusion?

17. Since you have been going back and forth, the length of time that you have spent in a foreign country does not amount to a year. To meet the bona fide resident test for a foreign country, you must have lived there for an uninterrupted period that includes an entire tax year; that is from January 1 through December 31. You must also make this country as your tax home. You fail to meet this test. Your purpose in the country is to work there and not to live there permanently. You do not want to run the risk of being audited and then losing the exclusion.

What is this tax form called the Foreign Bank Account Report? When do I submit the form?

18. You are required to fill out the Foreign Bank Account Report (Form TD F 90-22.1) to disclose accounts you hold in foreign banks and other financial institutions if your total balance of all accounts is $10,000 or greater at any point during the year. The form has to be submitted with the US Treasury Department by June 30, 2009. You will have to provide information on all your financial accounts held in a foreign country including bank accounts (checking and savings), investment accounts, mutual funds, retirement accounts, and securities and other brokerage accounts.

    The instructions for filling out Form TD F 90-22.1 state that every US citizen or resident alien, partnership, corporation, estate, or trust must file TD F 90-22.1 if they have "financial interest in or signature authority, or other authority over any financial accounts, including bank, securities, or other types of financial accounts in a foreign country, if the aggregate value of these financial accounts exceeds $10,000 at any time during the calendar year."

It is very important that your report must be received by the due date (June 30). The FBAR is not an income tax return and should not be mailed with any income tax returns. The FBAR must be filed on or before June 30 of the following year to: U.S. Department of the Treasury, P.O. Box 32621, Detroit, MI 48232-0621.

Penalties will be assessed for failing to file this report and as they are quite harsh, we recommend that you make the effort even if you missed the filing deadline.
There are exceptions to this rule. You do not need to report accounts held at US military banking facilities or if your banks are located in Guam, Puerto Rico, and the US Virgin Islands. There are also no need to report US-based accounts held by a branch or division of a foreign bank.

I am a New Yorker living in Czech Republic. I have always been paying taxes to the US. The first time I have heard of the Foreign Bank Account Report was last month. I heard that tough action is being threatened against those who do not file the form. What do I do now?

19. If you do not have sufficient time to get the information required for filing the FBAR on or before June 30, 2009, you should file the delinquent FBAR report as soon as possible. Attach a statement to explain why the report was filed late. Send a copy of this delinquent FBAR, along with a copy of the 2008 tax return, by Sept. 23, 2009, to the Philadelphia Offshore Identification Unit. Provided all your taxable income was reported, you will not be imposed a penalty for your failure to file on time.

    On June 24, 2009, the IRS offered the following advice: Taxpayers who reported and paid tax on all their 2008 taxable income, but only recently learned of their FBAR filing obligation and have insufficient time to gather the necessary information to complete the FBAR, should file the delinquent FBAR report according to the instructions and attach a statement explaining why the report is filed late.

I am an expat living in Italy. This is the first year that I will be required to pay taxes as a US citizen living in a foreign country. My employer has been generous enough to pay many of my expenses here, including the rent, utilities, education of my 2 kids, as well as insurance and taxes associated with my living here. Can I use these for exemptions? What is the maximum limit?

20. What you are referring to is the Foreign Earned Income Exclusion. The expenses you mentioned can be applied towards the foreign earned income exclusion up to the maximum amount for the year ($91,400 for 2010) as long as they were included in your taxable foreign earned income. The following expenses qualify for the exclusion: rent, Fair rental value of housing provided by your employer, repairs, utilities other than telephone, real property and personal property insurance (homeowners & renters insurance), occupancy taxes, nonrefundable security deposits or lease payments, furniture rental, residential parking fees, tax equalization payments paid by your employer, education expenses for your dependent children.

I have made a voluntary disclosure of my tax obligations and was asked to pay a 20% offshore penalty. Should I pay this penalty? Is it negotiable?

21. The 20% penalty is far less than the penalty if you do not follow the amnesty program, and is not negotiable for the most part. However, according to the New Foreign Bank Account Report (FBAR) FAQs issued by the IRS on June 25, 2009, if any part of the penalty structure is unacceptable to a taxpayer, that case will follow the standard audit process. All relevant years and issues will be subject to a complete examination. At the conclusion of the examination, all applicable penalties (including information return and FBAR penalties) will be imposed.

    The IRS added that these penalties may be greater than the 20% penalty initially calculated. You do not have any options if you want to get up to date with your responsibilities as a US taxpayer.

In have been paying taxes on time and in full ever since I became an expat. Last year, my financial situation worsened and I may be late in making tax payments. Which penalties incur interest? From what date does the interest accrue?

22. If you are referring to accuracy-related or delinquency penalties, interest is assessed from the due date of the tax return. For all other penalties, interest is computed from the date of assessment of the penalty.

    The failure-to-file penalty assesses a 5% charge on the U.S. tax due, up to a maximum amount of 25%. The failure-to-pay penalty equals one-half of 1% of the amount owed per month, maxing out at 25% as well. You will be charged interest on an unpaid balance at the prevailing rate. You may also have to pay a penalty for not paying sufficient estimated taxes. Keep in mind that the penalty for not filing at all is higher than the penalty for not paying on time and that by paying a partial amount; you can limit the penalty and interest charges.

23. I already pay taxes in Norway where I have been staying for the past 4 years. What can you tell me about foreign tax credit?

You can claim a credit for taxes that you have paid in a foreign country. Not included in this computation are the taxes paid on any income, which has been excluded from US taxation using the foreign earned income exclusion or the foreign housing exclusion. A tax credit is more valuable than a deduction since a tax credit reduces your liability on a dollar-for-dollar basis. Get your total foreign-source income and divide it by your total worldwide income. This resulting percentage, when multiplied with your US tax liability, must not exceed your foreign tax credit.

If your foreign tax credit is higher than your limit, you may be able to carry the excess credit over to the next year or you may even apply it to one of the previous two years.

Not all types of taxes qualify for the foreign tax credit. The IRS says that four qualifications have to be met. The tax should be imposed on you (and not the employer); the tax must be owed or already paid by you; the tax has to be legal; and the tax is based on income that you earned.

How Do I know if I have to file a state return?

23. In many cases, you will not need to file a State Income Tax Return; however, each State has its own rules and some states require you file a Tax Return even if you have moved abroad. We will check the rules for your state when preparing your Federal Return and let you know if you need to file a State Return.

Do I have to pay tax on a gift received from my foreign friend?

24. It depends on whether your friend is a US resident or not. If he, like yourself, is a US resident living in a foreign country, then gift rules are the same as for US gift - you do not pay tax on any gift amount and the giver pays gift tax on the amount over $13,000 (for 2011). If he is a non-US resident, then you are not paying tax but must report the gift to IRS if its value exceeds $100,000. Your friend, though, should consult the local tax specialist on what tax consequences his gift will have in that country. You can find more details at the IRS website (http://www.irs.gov/businesses/article/0,,id=200722,00.html).

I am an American living in the UK. How will the residence changes affect me?

25. Your residence position is based on how many days you physically spend in the UK (with every day you are in the UK at midnight being counted as a day for these purposes) as well as your longer term intentions. Any individual coming to the UK intending to stay for at least 3 years will be regarded as resident and ordinarily resident in the UK from the date they arrive. If you are only intending to stay for between 2 and 3 years it is possible you could be regarded as resident but not ordinarily resident as long as you abide by certain rules such as not purchasing a property in the UK. If you come to the UK intending to stay less than 2 year your residence position would be based on the number of days spent in the UK, as long as you were physically present here for less than 183 days in any tax year (UK tax years run from 6 April to 5 April) you would not be regarded as resident in the UK.

    Your residence position is important when considering how foreign income is taxed in the UK while your UK earned income is taxed in the UK regardless of your residence position.

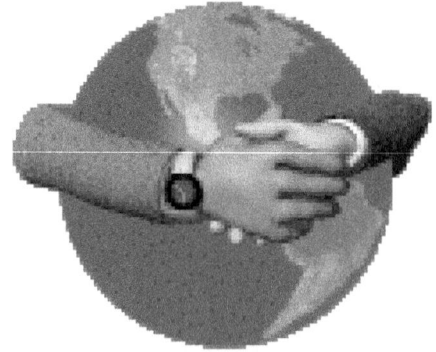

FBAR

Important Newsbreak for Expats Who Just Found Out About FBAR and are Considering joining OVDI
If you are an American citizen who is considering joining the 2011 Offshore Voluntary Disclosure Initiative, you need to talk to us about it first. The government is only giving a pass at filing delinquent FBARs without a penalty to those who have already reported and paid back taxes.

In this section:
Do You Have a Foreign Financial Account?
If you own or have authority over a foreign financial account, including a bank account, brokerage account, mutual fund, unit trust, or other types of financial accounts, you may be required to report the account yearly to the Internal Revenue Service. Under the Bank Secrecy Act, each United States person must file a Report of Foreign Bank and Financial Accounts (FBAR), if

- The person has a financial interest in, or signature authority (or other authority that is comparable to signature authority) over one or more accounts in a foreign country and
- The aggregate value of all foreign financial accounts exceeds $10,000 at any time during the calendar year.

The FBAR is required because foreign financial institutions may not be subject to the same reporting requirements as domestic financial institutions. The FBAR is a tool to help the United States government identify persons who may be using foreign financial accounts to circumvent United States law. Investigators use FBARs to help identify or trace funds used for illegal purposes or to identify unreported income kept or earned abroad.

Who Must File an FBAR
United States Person: Under this definition, the term "United States person" means (1) a citizen or resident of the United States, (2) a domestic partnership, (3) a domestic corporation, or (4) a domestic estate or trust.

Reporting and Filing Information
A person who holds a foreign financial account may have a reporting obligation even though the account produces no taxable income. Checking the appropriate block on FBAR-related federal income tax return questions (found on Form 1040 of Schedule B, the "Other Information" section of Form 1041, Schedule B of Form 1065, and Schedule N of Form 1120) and filing Form TD F 90-22.1, Report of Foreign Bank and Financial Accounts, satisfies the account holder's reporting obligation (Description of all IRS forms can be found on our site).

The FBAR is not meant to be filed with the filer's federal income tax return. The granting, by the IRS, of an extension to file Federal income tax returns does not extend the due date for filing an FBAR. You may not request an extension for filing the FBAR. The FBAR must be received by the IRS on or before June 30 of the following year. Account holders who do not comply with the FBAR reporting requirements may be subject to civil penalties, criminal penalties, or both.

Exceptions to the Reporting Requirement
Exceptions to the reporting requirement can be found in the FBAR Instructions. These exceptions include:

- Accounts in U.S. military banking facilities operated by a United States financial institution to serve U.S. Government installations abroad are not considered to be accounts in a foreign country for purposes of the reporting requirement.
- An officer or employee of a bank that is subject to the supervision of the Comptroller of the Currency, the Board of Governors of the Federal Reserve System, the Office of Thrift Supervision, or the Federal Deposit Insurance Corporation, is not required to report having signature or other authority over a foreign account if the officer or employee has no personal interest in the account.
- An officer or employee of a domestic corporation whose equity securities are listed on a national securities exchange or which has assets exceeding $10 million and 500 or more shareholders of record, is not required to report having signature or other authority over a foreign account if the person has no personal financial interest in the account, and the officer or employee has been advised in writing by the chief financial officer of the corporation that the corporation has filed a current report that includes the foreign account.
- More information about Foreign Bank Account Reporting can be found on the IRS web page: FAQs Regarding Report of Foreign Bank and Financial Accounts (FBAR) and Filing Requirements. This link also provides details on various forms of foreign financial accounts and explains how to file FBARs for prior years or amend a previously filed FBAR.
- There is a temporary exception on FBAR rules for NON-US Persons. Please see IRS Announcement 2009-51 dated June 5, 2009 regarding a temporary exception of FBAR rules for non-US persons.

About the Form TD F 90.22.1
- The deadline is an ARRIVAL deadline, not a proof of mailed by deadline.
- If you have multiple accounts that require more than one page, the full form and instructions can be found on the IRS website. If you only require the basic single account version of the form, fill out only the first page.

Fine-Print IRS Details Regarding FBAR
Further details published by the IRS regarding FBAR can be found at: Workbook on the Report of Foreign Bank and Financial Accounts (FBAR). This document includes details on fines and penalties; they are not pretty.

What the Wall Street Journal Says:
See the latest information on FBARs as reported on July 20th, 2009 in the WSJ: IRS Gets Tougher on Offshore Tax Evaders. This gives you a sense of the government's attitude toward anyone having an offshore account; you are guilty until you prove you are innocent.

Final Note
FBAR rules have become a major irritant, to be sure, but a fact of expat life. In fact, the government expanded compliance net extends to many more US persons than just expats. Make sure you know your status and your possibility of being required to file such reports.

We strongly suggest using FedEx, DHL or certified mail so you have proof of mailing and proof of arrival by the due date: June 30th of each year starting with tax year 2009.

FBAR - FAQ.

Important Newsbreak for Expats Who Just Found out about FBAR and are considering joining OVDI

If you are an American citizen who is considering joining the 2011 Offshore Voluntary Disclosure Initiative (http://www.irs.gov/newsroom/article/0,,id=234900,00.html), you need to talk to us about it first. The government is only giving a pass at filing delinquent FBARs without a penalty to **those who have already reported and paid back taxes.**

Q. What is a financial account?
A. A "financial account" includes any bank, securities, securities derivatives or other financial instruments accounts. The term includes any savings, demand, checking, deposit or any other account maintained with a financial institution or other person engaged in the business of a financial institution. Financial account also generally includes any accounts in which the assets are held in a commingled fund, and the account owner holds an equity interest in the fund (including mutual funds). Individual bonds, notes, or stock certificates held by the filer are not a financial account nor is an unsecured loan to a foreign trade or business that is not a financial institution.

Q. What is meant by the term "commingled funds?"
A. The reference to "commingled fund" appears in the definition of the term "financial account" in the FBAR instructions. The instructions state that the term "financial account" generally encompasses accounts in which the assets are held in a commingled fund and the account owner holds an equity interest in the fund.

Persons with a financial interest in, or signature authority over, a foreign commingled fund that is a mutual fund are required to file an FBAR unless another filing exception, as provided in the FBAR instructions or other relevant guidance, applies. The IRS will not interpret the term "commingled fund" as applying to funds other than mutual funds with respect to FBARs for calendar year 2009 and prior years. Thus, the IRS will not apply its enforcement authority adversely in the case of persons with a financial interest in, or signature authority over, any other foreign commingled fund with respect to that account for calendar year 2009 and earlier calendar years, including hedge funds and private equity funds. Notice 2010-23 (http://www.irs.gov/pub/irs-drop/n-10-23.pdf)

Q. Is an FBAR required for accounts maintained with financial institutions located in a foreign country if the accounts hold noncash assets, such as gold?
A. Yes. An account with a financial institution that is located in a foreign country is a financial account for FBAR purposes whether the account holds cash or non-monetary assets.

Q. What does "maximum value of account" mean (for Box 15 on the FBAR)?
A. The maximum value of account is the largest amount (not the average amount) of currency and nonmonetary assets that appear on any quarterly or more frequent account statements issued for the applicable year. If periodic account statements are not issued, the maximum account value is the largest amount of currency or nonmonetary assets in the account at any time during the year. Convert foreign currency by using the official

exchange rate at the end of the year.

Though the FBAR instructions direct filers to use the official exchange rate, the Internal Revenue Service has no official exchange rate and generally accepts any posted exchange rate that is used consistently. For exchange rates, check the U.S. Treasury Web site (http://www.fms.treas.gov/intn.html#rates) or other commercial sites.

Q. A person owns foreign financial accounts X, Y and Z with maximum account balances of $100, $12,000 and $3,000, respectively. Does the person have to file an FBAR and if so, which accounts must be listed on the FBAR?
A. The FBAR instructions require the filing of the FBAR form " ... if the aggregate value of these financial accounts exceeds $10,000 at any time during the calendar year ... " In this scenario, the person has an FBAR filing obligation because the aggregate value of foreign financial accounts X, Y and Z is $15,100. The person must report foreign financial accounts X, Y and Z on the FBAR even though accounts X and Z have maximum account values below $10,000.

Q. A person owns foreign financial accounts A, B and C with account balances of $3,000, $1,000 and $8,000, respectively. Does the person have to file an FBAR and if so, which accounts must be listed on the FBAR?
A. Even though no single account is over $10,000, because the aggregate value of accounts A, B and C is over $10,000, the person has to file an FBAR and must report foreign financial accounts A, B and C on the FBAR.

Q. Is an FBAR required if the account generates neither interest nor dividend income?
A. Yes, an FBAR must be filed whether or not the foreign account generates any income.

Q. Does the term "other authority over a financial account" mean that a person, who has the power to direct how an account is invested but who cannot make disbursements to the accounts, has to file an FBAR?
A. No, an FBAR is not required because the person has no power of disposition of money or other property in the account.

Q. Must a U.S. person file an FBAR to report a Eurodollar account in the Cayman Islands?
A. Yes, the Cayman Islands account is a foreign account.

Q. A New York corporation owns a foreign company that has foreign accounts. The corporation will file an FBAR for the foreign company's accounts. Do the primary owners of the U.S. Company also have to file?
A. Yes, if any owner directly or indirectly owns more than 50 percent of the total value of the shares of stock, that owner will have to file an FBAR.

Q. A company has more than 25 foreign accounts. What should they enter in Part ll of the FBAR?
A. If the filer holds a financial interest in more than 25 accounts, check the yes box in item 14 and indicate the number of accounts in the space provided. Do not

complete any further items in Part II or Part III of the report. Sign the form in item 44/45 and enter the date signed in item 46. Any person who lists more than 25 accounts in item 14 must provide all the information called for in Part II and Part III when requested by the Department of the Treasury.

Q. What are the exceptions to the FBAR filing requirement?
A. Accounts in U.S. military banking facilities, operated by a United States financial institution to serve U.S. government installations abroad, are not considered as accounts in a foreign country. For this reason, these accounts do not have to be reported on an FBAR.

An officer or employee of a bank that is subject to the supervision of the Comptroller of the Currency, the Board of Governors of the Federal Reserve System, the Office of Thrift Supervision, or the Federal Deposit Insurance Corporation need not report that he has signature or other authority over a foreign bank, securities or other financial account maintained by the bank, if the officer or employee has NO personal financial interest in the account.

An officer or employee of a domestic corporation whose equity securities are listed on a national securities exchange or which has assets exceeding $10 million and 500 or more shareholders of record, need not file a report concerning signature authority over a foreign financial account of the corporation, if he has NO personal financial interest in the account and he has been advised, in writing, by the chief financial officer of the corporation that the corporation has filed a current report, which includes that account.

FATCHT & Form 8938

In recent years, the IRS and US Treasury have stepped up their efforts toward tracking down delinquent tax payers and enforcing payment of overdue taxes. One of these initiatives has been labeled the "Foreign Account Tax Compliance Act". FATCA is part of the Hiring Incentives to Restore Employment (HIRE) Act, which was designed to enforce higher tax compliance among U.S. taxpayers with foreign accounts and assets. FATCA created Form 8938, an additional foreign account reporting requirement **over and above the Report of Foreign Bank and Financial Accounts (FBAR)** or **Form TD F 90-22.1** that needs to be filed with the U.S. Treasury every year. If a taxpayer has more than a certain amount of foreign assets, Form 8938 is included as part of their annual 1040 filing and requires reporting an expanded list of foreign assets not covered by FBAR.

Every expat should be made aware of FATCA and how it may affect their investments and taxes.

How FATCA Will Affect Me?

The purpose of the FATCA is to force managers of foreign financial institutions to report all American clients to the IRS or be severely penalized with high withholding taxes. If the information reported is not 100% accurate and complete, the fund manager will still be faced with a penalty. This rule, however, is not without complications:

- Some countries have data protection laws in place that would be if the manager cooperates with the IRS.
- A fund manager may not realize that he has an American client because the client is represented by a non-American.
- The client may not provide the manager with the required information.

The penalty is solely applied to the manager, not the American client, regardless of the manager's nationality. As you see, a non-cooperative American expat client may be more trouble than he is worth.

Who Must File Form 8938

U.S. Citizens Living Abroad:
For U.S. citizens who are considered by the IRS to be foreign residents for the entire tax year or who meet the physical presence test for living in a foreign county, the new limits are:

- **Single**: Aggregate foreign assets of USD 200,000 on the last day of the year or USD 300,000 at any time during the year.
- **Married Filing Jointly**: Aggregate foreign assets of USD 400,000 on the last day of the year or USD 600,000 at any time during the year.

Why Should Foreign Fund Managers Comply?

You may wonder why a foreign fund manager would cooperate with the IRS even though they do not (most of them) have any ties to the US government. The answer is simple: the penalty. Fund managers normally feel obligated to register because the American bond and equity markets are the largest in the world.

"The law requires that foreign financial institutions (a category that seems to include everybody from financial advisers to pension funds) register with the Internal Revenue Service by June 30th 2013. If they do not register, they will then be regarded as "non-participating". In that case a 30% withholding tax will be applied to all their income on American assets from 2014 as well as to the proceeds from the sales of these assets from 2015."

Can Americans Invest Abroad with FATCA in Place?

FATCA may cause fund managers to deal differently with American clients if it goes through congress unchanged. It is in the best interest of international financial institutions (and, thusly, American investors) that the initiative will be adjusted in such a way that fund managers can continue to work with American clients. Currently, the steep withholding taxes will force many international fund managers to deny Americans or avoid all American assets, which puts both at a disadvantage.

Some Other Considerations:

- Form 8938 is due at the time of your normal tax filing including extensions.
- Filing Form 8938 does not exempt you from the requirement to file Form TD 90-22.1, the Report of Foreign Bank and Financial Accounts (FBAR).
- If you are not required to file a tax return, you do not need to file Form 8938.
- If you are required to file a Form 8938 and you have a specified foreign financial asset reported on Form 3520, Form 3520-A, Form 5471, Form 8621, Form 8865, or Form 8891 (http://crevelingandcreveling.us1.list-manage.com/track/click?u=2e06a9353545b67d7087e31d2&id=0a41054168&e=2301efec5a), you do not need to report the asset on Form 8938. On the Form 8938, however, you do have to identify which and how many of each of these forms you file.
- Even if a foreign financial asset is reported on one of the forms listed above, it still must be included it in your calculation of specified foreign financial assets.
- The penalty for failing to file Form 8938 is USD 10,000, with an additional penalty up to $50,000 for continued failure to file after IRS notification. A 40% penalty on any understatement of tax attributable to non-disclosed assets can also be imposed and special statute of limitation rules apply.

Form 8938 is separate from the FBAR form and its requirements. The FBAR (90-22.1) is filed with the US treasury while Form 8938 is filed with the IRS. However, if you are required to file Form 8938, your assets will most likely fall under the FBAR filing requirements (f the majority of your assets are financial) accounts.

Penalties

Ignorance is not bliss when it comes to anything tax related, and there are penalties for failing to file the appropriate forms by the appropriate date. Each penalty is levied on a case by case basis, however, and those who are ignorant are usually not penalized as harshly as those who have intended to (or appear to have intended to) defraud the government. The penalty that may be incurred for failing to file Form 8938 is a severe $10,000 with an additional $50,000 for those who ignore the IRS's initial warning.

Additionally, the IRS may apply a 40% penalty on the taxes from non-disclosed assets.

Unlike many expat tax matters, the filing requirements leave little guess work. Everything is clearly detailed in the section "Form 8938 instructions" on the IRS website. These details include relevant dates, asset types, account types and thresholds.

Failing to comply or fully understand the 8938 requirements is a costly mistake, both in time and money. For questions and concerns regarding any aspect of your expat taxes, please contact the professionals at Taxes for Expats today.

The IRS continues to roll out new ways to identify Americans holding financial and investment accounts abroad. These disclosure reporting requirements all come loaded with the highest IRS penalties, starting at $10,000 per non-filing or incorrect filing incident.

Some Frequently Asked Questions about FATCA
What's a specified foreign financial asset?
For this definition we can go straight to the source - the IRS text:

- Any financial account maintained by a foreign financial institution.
- Other foreign financial assets, which include any of the following assets that are held for investment and not held in an account maintained by a financial institution.
- Stock or securities issued by someone other than a U.S. person,
- Any interest in a foreign entity, and
- Any financial instrument or contract that has an issuer or counterparty that is other than a U.S. person.

What are the value thresholds?
The aggregate value thresholds of specified foreign financial accounts vary depending on how you file your tax return.

Filing Status: Unmarried/Single
Aggregate Value at Year End: $50,000
Highest Aggregate Value at Any Time During the Year: $100,000
Filing Status: Married Filing Joint
Aggregate Value at Year End: $100,000
Highest Aggregate Value at Any Time During the Year: $200,000
Filing Status: Married Filing Separate
Aggregate Value at Year End: $50,000
Highest Aggregate Value at Any Time During the Year: $100,000
Filing Status: Taxpayer Living Abroad (Non-Joint)
Aggregate Value at Year End: $200,000
Highest Aggregate Value at Any Time During the Year: $400,000
Filing Status: Taxpayer Living Abroad (Joint)
Aggregate Value at Year End: $400,000
Highest Aggregate Value at Any Time During the Year: $600,000

If I'm currently filing the FBAR (TD F90-22.1) does Form 8938 replace it?

NO. Both forms are required to be filed. The FBAR will still be filed directly with the Treasury Department. The 8938 will be attached to your U.S. tax return and filed with the IRS.

What happens if the IRS finds out I didn't file or if I under-reported my foreign interest, dividends, capital gains, and business earnings?

If you don't file a complete and correct Form 8938, it is an automatic $10,000 penalty that can grow to a $50,000 penalty if not dealt with immediately. You will be required to pay the regular tax that would have been due on these assets plus interest and incur an additional penalty of 40% of the tax due. Don't forget there may be criminal penalties for non-compliance.

What Else should I know?

Form 8938 is required to be attached to your U.S. income tax return, but only required if you would otherwise be required to file a U.S. income tax return. So, if you are not required to file a U.S. tax return, you are not required to file form 8938 with it.

Do I have to report a specified foreign financial asset on Form 8938 if I report it on other IRS disclosure forms?

Maybe not. Please see a qualified tax professional to help you determine if you need to file form 8938. Remember, failure to file a correct and complete Form 8938 may result in $10,000 or more in penalties.

For most American expats, the annual filing of their U.S. tax return is not the real issue to worry about – it's the required disclosure reporting! Some of the most draconian IRS penalties are associated with the non-filing or incorrect filing of the various disclosure reports that you need to file if you hold foreign investments, foreign bank accounts, or foreign business interests. Don't risk losing your hard-earned international financial accounts to IRS penalties, work with a tax professional experienced in the international reporting requirements.

Asset Disclosure OVDI

If you missed the September 9, 2011 deadline for the IRS Offshore Voluntary Disclosure Initiative (OVDI) you should not bury your head in the sand and hope that the problem will go away (it won't). Fortunately a number of alternatives are available.

If you are a US Citizen or permanent resident and have not filed all your past returns and other forms required for reporting of foreign assets (such as 5471, FBAR, Form 8865, etc.), you can still take required steps to avoid large penalties or even criminal prosecution if the IRS finds you first. Doug Shulman - the IRS Commissioner - has gone on record stating that the IRS plans to pursue all taxpayers who are not filing appropriate offshore asset reporting forms: ""The time to comply with the U.S. tax code is now, as the risks of hiding money offshore keep rising."

One venue available is the IRS traditional Offshore Disclosure program which has always been and is still available: http://www.irs.gov/newsroom/article/0,,id=216678,00.html. If you come forward yourself, the Investigation Division will most likely decide there is no criminal action required against you. After that, they will send your returns to the audit division for review and possible imposition of penalties.

Another venue is to file your past tax returns together with the foreign asset reporting forms using regular filing procedures and hope the IRS does not discover you are filing the foreign asset reporting forms late. If you are discovered they may audit those returns and threaten to impose severe penalties. The penalties that may be imposed (even though they are rare) are explained on this page of our site: IRS Tax Penalties (http://www.taxesforexpats.com/expat-tax-advice/IRS-tax-penalties.html).

If you are still considering whether you should come clean to the IRS, you need to educate yourself about FATCA. This is a new act that came into effect on March 18, 2010. It will require foreign financial institutions - banks, brokers, pension funds, insurance companies - to report to the IRS all their clients who are U.S. persons.

It will come in full force in January 1, 2013. This will allow IRS to cross-check the list of people who have filed FBAR and those who must but did not. All institutions that do not comply will have a 30% withholding tax imposed on all their transactions concerning U.S. securities. In addition, FATCA will require that any foreign company not listed on a stock exchange or any foreign partnership which has 10% U.S. ownership to report to the IRS the names and tax I.D. number (TIN) of any U.S. owner.

You can read more about FATCA here:

- http://www.forbes.com/sites/robertwood/2011/10/24/oh-canada-hating-fbars-and-fatca/
- www.ey.com/Publication/vwLUAssets/Br_Fatca_2010/$FILE/FATCA_2010_English.pdf
- http://www.irs.gov/businesses/corporations/article/0,,id=236664,00.html
- http://www.deloitte.com/view/en_US/us/Services/tax/930c9948e681a210VgnVCM100000ba42f00aRCRD.htm

What is the takeaway? If you are a US citizen with a foreign financial account, the institution will be required by law to report on you to the IRS in a year's time.

PFIC Investment Co.'s

PFIC - Passive Foreign Investment Companies

Most tax related issues are complicated, and very few tax penalties are what some might call lenient. However, regulations for PFIC (Passive Foreign Investment Companies) put the rest to shame. It's unfortunate when a expat thinks he's coming to us for a simple tax return only to find that his investment in a non-US mutual fund changed the entire game plan. It would be nearly impossible to cover all the ins and outs of PFIC in a readable article, but what follows will provide a brief overview.

History

PFIC regulations came about as part of the 1986 Tax Reform Act. The purpose was to create an even playing field for US funds. Before the enactment of the Tax Reform Act, US mutual funds were required to pass all investment income to investors while foreign funds were allowed to shelter taxable income. Post Tax Reform Act, the advantage foreign funds had over US funds was obsolete, because it imposed penalties on all funds that would delay distribution. As a way of enforcing this new principle, the IRS obligates PFIC shareholders to report undistributed earnings and select one of three ways in which they would like them to be taxed.

- **Section 1291 Fund**
- **Mark to Market Election**
- **Qualified Election Fund**

The ABCs

First, it will be helpful to define exactly what a PFIC actually is. PFICs have...

- A 75% or greater percentage of the funds income is passive (meaning it comes through interest, capital gains, etc.)
- a 50% or greater percentage of the fund's holdings are held back to create passive income.

There are a few PFICs that are exceptions but most will fall within the confines of the above rules. In general, foreign mutual funds, money markets and pension funds are good examples of passive foreign investment companies. If a company (real estate, for example) has passive investments, it will be subject to PFIC rules unless it was set up as a corporation.

Taxation Methods
Section 1291 Fund

If the taxpayer does not choose a method of taxation, Section 1291 will be chosen for him.

Under this particular regime, prior year's "excess distributions" are taxed at the highest rate possible for the relevant years. Underpayment interest will also be collected.

Under 1291, the current year's excess are included as "other income" on the standard US tax return.

In contrast, the current year "excess distributions" are added to the "Other income" line of one's personal tax return. For the purposes of this election an "excess distributions" are either:

- The part of the distribution received from a section 1291 fund in the current tax year that is greater than 125% of the average distributions received in respect to such stock by the shareholder during the 3 preceding tax years (or, if shorter, the portion of the shareholder's holding period before the current tax year; or
- Any capital gains that result from the sale of PFIC shares

To add to the complexity- excess distributions that are taken (in either of the two aforementioned forms) must be allocated ratably over every year since the most recent excess distribution was taken (if any). Furthermore, all dividends are still required to be reported on Schedule B of the income tax return but any capital gains or losses do not get reported on Schedule D.

To provide an illustration:

1 share of XYZ Inc. (a foreign mutual fund) that was purchased for $100,000 on January 1, 2008. It distributed $8,000 of dividends on July 4 of each year. On December 31, 2010, the share was sold for $400,000. Since the dividends for each year never exceeded the prior year's amount, there are no excess distributions relating to the dividends. However, since the sale resulted in a capital gain of 100,000, the gain is an excess distribution and will be allocated ratably of each day the share was held. In particular, the excess distributions would result in $100,000 being allocated to 2008 and 2009 and taxed at the highest marginal tax rate (35% in 2008 and 2009). Also, interest would be charged to both years for the amount owed as of the due date for the particular tax year's tax return- i.e. interest would accrue from April 15, 2009 for the 2008 excess distribution tax). Finally, the allocation of excess distribution for 2010 would be added to ordinary income line of the income tax return (line 21 for those filing Form 1040). Assuming the taxpayer was in the 33% income tax bracket for 2010, the additional tax caused by the PFIC regime would exceed $120,000. Please note that the transaction will not be recorded on the taxpayer's Schedule D and that the dividends, though not taxed as part of the excess distribution regime, would still need to be reported on the taxpayer's schedule B as non-qualified dividends.

To have perspective on the degree of additional taxation that can occur with the Excess Distribution method- if the $300,000 gain listed in the aforementioned scenario would have come from the sale of a non-PFIC, the tax would have been $45,000 (almost a third of the total PFIC tax liability). As you can clearly see- the IRS wants to discourage investing in foreign mutual funds.

QEF Election (Qualifying Electing Fund)

A second, simpler option for shareholders of PFICs is the QEF election. A first glance, it would appear to be a much better option for most investors since effectively results in the PFIC being treated like a US based mutual fund- the ordinary and capital gains income of the PFIC separately flow through to the shareholder according to percentage of ownership. For example, a taxpayer with a 1% stake in a PFIC that earns $100,000 in ordinary income and another $50,000 in capital gains income will report $1,000 as "other income" on the tax return while $500 will be reported on Schedule D.

However, there is one huge obstacle to making this election- most PFICs are unable to be classified as a QEF since the IRS demands that a QEF comply with IRS reporting requirements (a large request for a non-US based company). Consequently, the QEF election is not frequently available.

Mark-to-Market Election

The third option available to PFIC shareholders is to make a mark-to-market election. This method allows the shareholder to report the annual gain in market value (i.e. unrealized gain) of the PFIC shares as ordinary income on the "other income" line of their tax returns. Unrealized losses are only reportable to the extent that gains have been previously reported. The adjusted basis for PFIC stock must include the gains and losses previously reported as ordinary income. Upon the sale of the PFIC shares, all gains are reported as ordinary income whereas losses are reported on Schedule D.

To choose this method, the PFIC generally must be traded on a major international stock exchange and can only apply to the current and future tax years.

Also, this election is independent of prior PFIC elections (i.e. QEF or Sect 1291 election). for example: If stock X was purchased in 2007 for $100, has a FMV on 12/31/11 of $120, and no PFIC forms were filed until 2011 (when Sect 1296- Mark-to-market- election was made), no PFIC filings would be needed for the prior years as long distributions were less than 125% and no capital gains occurred. For the current year, 8621 would be filed using Mark to market and the ordinary income would be $20.

State Taxes Liability

As a U.S. expatriate, you may assume that you have cut ties with your U.S. home and are not obligated to file a state return alongside your federal return (as all expats still have to do). This is not always true, however. And in the case of a few states, avoiding the state tax, even after years of living abroad, may seem almost impossible. In order to escape the state tax, there are several things you must do. It's important to complete these tasks **before** moving overseas.

The "Cool" Nine

Out of fifty states, there are only nine that make moving overseas and avoiding the state tax an easy task. This is due to the fact that Wyoming, Washington, Texas, South Dakota, Nevada, Florida and Alaska do not collect state income tax from their residents (and, by extension, expatriates from the state). Tennessee and New Hampshire only collect taxes on interest and dividends, so they also make life easy for expatriates.

Moving from any of these nine states is relatively easy, at least at it pertains to your federal tax return. These states allow you to move and work overseas without being taxed back home (on the state level). Because earned income is not taxed in these states, it is wise to move overseas from any of the favorable nine, whenever it is possible. Moving to one of these states before moving overseas should be considered as it will save you from having to file a state return and paying state taxes along with your federal taxes.

The 4 Unfavorable States

If your current state of residence is New Mexico, Virginia, South Carolina or California, the news is not as good. The governments of these states view their taxpayers as a needed asset. They will fight to hold on to every penny of owed tax. When leaving these states, it is up to you to prove (to the satisfaction of the state), that you will not be returning. If you cannot sufficiently prove this, you will be required to file a state return alongside your federal expatriate return.

If you are planning to return to your home state at some point, you will probably not be able to prove otherwise. South Carolina and California are the most diligent when it comes to finding ties that suggest future residency. You will most likely have to file a state tax return if the state government can locate any of the following ties:

- Telephone and/or utility bills
- Voter registration
- Library card
- Mailing address
- Association memberships
- In state dependents
- Property mortgage or lease
- State driver's license
- State investments or bank accounts

If it is important to you that you are not required to file a state tax return once you move overseas, you will need to cut all ties with your U.S. state before moving. To sufficiently end your residency with any of these "stubborn four," it is recommended to first transfer your residency to a more amenable state (preferably the Favorable Nine) before moving overseas. This transfer of residency must be thorough, however. If, for example, you still own property in one of the stubborn states, the state government will assume you are planning to return. And if you are still generating income within these states (New Mexico, Virginia, South Carolina or California) you will always be required to file a state return and pay taxes on this income.

Neutral States

The remaining states (thirty-seven) are neither favorable nor unfavorable. The majority of these states will release you from residency status if you have been gone for more than six months (though you will have to prove residency elsewhere). Proving your overseas residency should not be overly difficult, however, once you have settled in your new home.

Separating yourself from the Burden of a State Return

When planning to move overseas, there are usually many months of planning involved. During these months, you should also be sure to prepare for your new life as it pertains to tax issues. By taking the time to plan, you can sufficiently release yourself from the burden of filing a state return. For most expats, this benefit far outweighs the difficulty of forethought and tedious planning. The "simplest" solution is to relocate to a favorable state before heading overseas. You cannot simply stopover in one of these states, however. If this is your chosen course of action, you should plan to move months, even a full year, before picking up and moving abroad. Keep in mind that leaving dependents or property in any state but the favorable nine (especially the more stubborn states) will keep you tied to that state. Without physical ties to a stubborn state, a paper trail (bills, driver's license, etc.) will still allow the state government to claim you as a resident.

Expatriates are used to planning, and planning is also the key to minimizing your taxes as an expat. If you have not taken the proper precautions, keep in mind that you will be required to file a state return alongside your expat federal return (whether or not you think you should actually owe state taxes).

Required Documents

As an expat, preparing your taxes can feel overwhelming. However, If you take your time and go through each step of the process thoroughly, you can avoid most of the pain normally attributed to it. When you visit your expat tax preparer, it is important to have all the necessary documentation ready. This article will outline what documents you should prepare to make this process simple and straightforward.

I. Basic Information

A. Tax Questionnaire
Before filing your return, your expat tax preparer will ask you to complete a questionnaire. On this form, you will provide basic identifying information and information about your dependents. Additionally, you will answer questions about other activities that relate to expatriates. It is important to read and answer each of these questions carefully, not assuming anything. Any misinformation on this questionnaire will greatly slow down the rest of the process.

B. Last Year's Return
If you filed last year, it is extremely important to provide your tax preparer with last year's form. Your expat tax professional will want to cross reference your current information with previous information and be made aware of drastic changes. Additionally, he or she will look for deductions that were previously overlooked. When filing online, information on last year's form is essential.

C. Calendar of Travel Dates
If you travel back and forth between the U.S. and your foreign home, it is essential to know how many days are spent stateside and how many are spent overseas. Your taxable income and relevant deductions are affected by these numbers. To determine residency and whether or not you qualify for the Foreign Earned Income Exclusion, keeping an accurate travel calendar is key.

II. Income

A. Compensation, Wages and/or Tips
It is essential that you provide all W-2, P60, P45 and any other wage reporting forms. For self-employed expats, provide accurate and detailed records of all earnings and deductions. Some foreign countries do not have income taxes. In such cases, you will need to keep careful records (and save bank statements or check stubs) on your own for the purpose of reporting to the IRS.

B. Interest/Dividend Income
Any income generated through interest or dividends will be reported on Form 1099 (or the foreign equivalent). You must provide this information to your tax preparer, even if the account was closed within the year. Each

interest earning account will require its own form, so be sure you have received them all before filing.

C. Securities and Stocks
At the end of every year, your broker will send you a statement detailing all stocks and securities that were purchased or sold that year. This information is important for your tax preparation as an expat. Before providing your tax preparer with this statement, be sure that it outlines the purchase price, transaction fee, purchase/sale date (as these details are relevant to your tax return).

D. Real Estate
Any real estate purchased or sold is relevant to your expat tax forms. Your tax provider will need to know the purchase price as well as the transaction date. Rental property income (and expenses relevant for deductions) should also be included on your expat tax forms.

E. Distributions (including Pensions, Annuities, Profit Sharing Plans and IRA)
It is also important to provide your preparer with information about withdrawals from your IRA, pensions or other retirement accounts. In such cases, your employer's financial institution will normally mail a 1099-R (or the foreign equivalent). Include this form in the paperwork provided to your preparer. Additionally, Social Security benefits are reported on Form 1099-SSA. This form should also be provided to your preparer. Be sure to enlist an international tax expert when preparing your expat taxes, as some countries have agreements with the IRS (regarding Social Security), and these agreement can have a significant effect on your taxes.

F. Other Income
Partnership, trust or business interest is usually reported on the Schedule K-1 (or the foreign equivalent). Provide this form to your preparer. Unemployment income is reported on Form 1099- G. Don't forget to use Form 1099-MISC to report any miscellaneous income not covered in the previous sections. Child support and alimony must also be reported.

III. Deductions
A. Interest & Taxes Paid
Under the expatriate tax rules, interest paid on a home mortgage or student loan will earn you deductions. In addition, property taxes and foreign income taxes are examples of deductions that may be claimed through taxes paid. You must be able to prove interest paid and deductible taxes, however, so it is important to keep accurate records and provide this proof to your preparer.

B. Foreign Housing Expenses
Certain expats are allowed to deduct a portion of their overseas housing expenses. If you qualify, your preparer will need all of the financial details of

your housing situation.

C. Dependents
Just as it is with in-country taxes, children and dependents result in deductions and credits for expats. You must provide information on all of your dependents (including child care expenses). If you are paying for your children's higher education, this may also result in deductions and credits. All of this information should be provided to your preparer.

D. Other Deductions
Gifts to family members, business expenses that were never reimbursed, alimony and child support payments, medical expenses, donations to charity, etc. are all things to bring up (and provide documentation for) when speaking with your preparer. These are expenses that usually result in deductions.

IV. Other requirements
A. Foreign Bank Accounts
Foreign banks accounts are not irrelevant to your taxes as an expat. In fact, if your foreign accounts meet or exceed $10,000 (combined) on any given day during the year, you must report this amount to the IRS by June 30th of each relevant year. This amount is reported via Form 90-22.1 (Foreign Bank and Accounts Report) and is filed separately from your expat tax return.

B. Conclusion
Each document mentioned in this article is important to the correct filing of your taxes. If you cannot locate one of these forms (and it applies to you), contact your employer or financial institution and ask them to resend the form. Any omission will be noticed by the IRS, and will therefore result in an audit. It is much easier and wiser to simply do things right the first time.

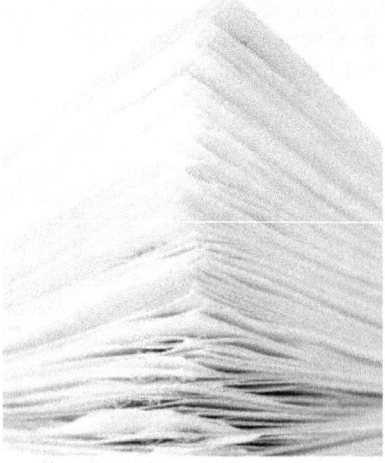

www.blogs.princeton.edu

Tax Bracket

Your tax bracket is the rate you pay on the "last dollar" you earn; but as a percentage of your income, your tax rate is generally less than that. First, here are the tax rates and the income ranges where they apply:

Tax Year:	[2011 /]
Filing Status:	[Single /]
If your taxable income is between…	**your tax bracket is:**
0 and 8,500	10 %
8,500 and 34,500	15 %
34,500 and 83,600	25 %
83,600 and 174,400	28 %
174,400 and 379,150	33 %
379,150 and above	35 %

To take an example, suppose your taxable income (after deductions and exemptions) was exactly $100,000 in 2008 and your status was married filing separately; then your tax would be calculated like this:

($ 8,025 minus	0)	x .10	$ 802.50
(32,550 minus	8,025)	x .15	3,678.75
(65,725 minus	32,550)	x .25	8,293.75
(100,000 minus	65,725)	x .28	9,597.00
Total:	$ 22,372.00		

This puts you in the 28% tax bracket, since that's the highest rate applied to any of your income; but as a percentage of the whole $100,000, your tax is about 22.37%.

"Taxable Income" here is really Regularly Taxed Income minus Adjustments, Deductions, and Exemptions. Payroll Tax (Social Security and Medicare), and Qualified Dividends and Long Term Capital Gains are separate calculations. See this Tax Calculator for more.

Tax Hikes, Tax Cuts

1993 saw a tax hike on the wealthy (via two new brackets at the top), and then 2001 through 2003 saw a series of tax cuts that lowered the tax brackets as follows:

1992	1993 - 2000	2001	2002	2003 - 2010	2011 - 2012	2013 ?
15%	15%	15%	10%	10%	Same as 2010	10%
			15%	15%		15%
28%	28%	27.5%	27%	25%		25%
31%	31%	30.5%	30%	28%		28%
	36%	35.5%	35%	33%		36%
	39.6%	39.1%	38.6%	35%		39.6%

From 2000 to 2002 most brackets dropped by one percent, and there was a new low bracket added for the "lucky ducky's" (http://www.opinionjournal.com/extra/?id=110002937) at the very bottom. In 2003 most brackets got an additional cut of two percent with a special gift for the "other" lucky ducky's, the ones at the top. But note that the rich still paid more in 2003, and everybody else paid less, than was the case in 1992. Now if we could just balance the budget...

Future Tax Rates

As of early 2009, the plan for the future was to leave the lower tax brackets alone, and raise the top two brackets to where they were during the 1990s. The cutoffs for the top brackets were to be raised, so that singles making above $200,000 annually, or families making above $250,000, would be the ones affected by the higher rates.

As of August 2010, Congress still hasn't made those changes legal. If Congress doesn't act before New Year's, all brackets will automatically revert to where they were in 2000, meaning **a big tax increase for everybody**. But hopefully Congress won't really do anything; they'll just follow the path of least political resistance, and temporarily freeze all brackets at their current levels until after the 2012 elections. (You heard it here first!)

(Update, December 2010: The prediction above came true! All tax brackets will be frozen through 2012.)

IRA Rules

U.S. workers usually save for retirement by contributing annually to either Roth or traditional IRA accounts. After moving overseas, it may not be possible to continue this practice. Many expats are ill-advised, however, because some accountants do not understand the complexities that surround an expat's tax life. As a result, you may have been advised to make unprofitable contributions to these accounts. This article addresses that problem, and what you should do if you have made contributions that your accountant should have advised against.

Qualifications for IRA Contribution
If you received taxable compensation during the year and you did not reach age seventy and a half by the end of the year; you are qualified to contribute to a traditional IRA. You can contribute to a Roth IRA if you received taxable compensation during the year, and, if your modified adjusted gross income falls below:

- $179,000 if you are married and filing jointly or are a qualifying widow or widower.
- $110,000 if you are married and filing separately (you must have lived with your spouse at some point during the year).
- $122,000 if you are single, or if you are married filing separately but did not reside with your spouse at any point during the year.

If you meet the above qualifications, you may contribute to the relevant IRA account assuming your taxable compensation is:

- Income earned from working in the U.S.
- Foreign income in excess of the Foreign Housing and Foreign Earned Income Exclusions.
- Income from a stateside job held before moving
- Income from a U.S. summer job
- Income allocable to U.S. business trips
- Compensation from the U.S. government (for government employees).
- Qualifying employer contributions

Taxable Compensation
To contribute to either IRA, you must receive taxable compensation. Taxable compensation is income earned through work. Money excluded from income, housing allowances and foreign earned income; for example, do not count as taxable compensation for the purpose of IRA accounts.

Modified Adjusted Gross Income
When determining whether or not you meet the qualifications for IRA contribution, it is your modified adjusted gross income that is considered. This AGI number is your income plus the amount deducted according to the Foreign Earned Income Exclusion.

Foreign Earned Income and Roth IRA Contributions
A Roth IRA is a vehicle for savings and can be established within the confines of an IRS approved institution (credit union, bank, brokerage house, etc.). A Roth IRA can be set up

at any point during the year, but funds must be contributed by the due date of your return for that year (not including extensions). Contributions are limited as the modified adjusted gross income increases. Qualifying income includes, but is not limited to, salaries; wages, income earned through self-employment, commissions, alimony, and deferred compensation. Qualifying income does not include the amount covered by the Foreign Earned Income Exclusion or the Housing Exclusion. Lastly, qualifying income must not be less that the Roth IRA contribution.

If You Have Made Unprofitable Contributions
Both the traditional IRA and the Roth IRA are helpful and valuable savings methods. However, it is vastly important to determine whether you continue to qualify for contribution after moving overseas. If you believe you have made ill-advised contributions, or if you simply wish to avoid making this mistake, contact the experts at Taxes for Expats. Our knowledgeable staff will examine your individual situation, in detail, to determine your best course of action and whether or not you qualify for continued IRA contribution.

Past Return Copies

There are quite a few reasons why someone might need access to a previous year's tax return. And unless you are highly organized, you might not be able to retrieve a copy from your personal filing cabinet. Never fear, though, because in cases involving mortgages, student loans and citizenship, one is usually only required to provide the basic information that can be found on a tax return transcript.

Transcripts - Free

Transcripts of tax returns are available for three years prior to date, and they include the majority of the line items from your original tax return. If you are asked to provide an "exact copy," a transcript will not suffice. If you are simply in need of the information from your original return, however, a transcript is an easy and free solution.

If changes were made to your return (by you or the IRS) after it was filed, neither an exact copy nor a transcript will contain the information you need. In this case, you should request not a tax return transcript but a transcript of your tax account.

You can request either a tax return or a tax account transcript via the IRS (800-829-1040). The automated message will guide you through the process. Or, you can request your transcript by filing out and mailing this IRS form. Through either method, you can expect to receive your transcript anywhere from ten to thirty days from the time the IRS receives your information.

Exact Copies - $57 Per Year

If you are required to obtain an exact copy or if you are past the three year margin allowed for transcripts, the IRS allows you to obtain exact copies of your past six years' returns for a fee of $57.00 per year. You may request and obtain exact copies of your completed returns (with attachments) by filing out and mailing this form. Your payment will be addressed to the United States Treasury. It is wise to allow up to sixty days to receive exact copies of your returns.

It might be important to keep in mind that if a return has been jointly filed, either spouse may request transcripts or exact copies without the other spouse's signature (even after divorce).

E-filing Your Return

Make your US Tax filing process as easy and hassle-free as possible is are goal at US-Taxman. That means processing all your tax documents online and e-filing your return. We appreciate that nobody wants to deal with the hassle of printing paper returns and trips to the post office.

We are **usually** able to file your tax return online but in certain cases (due to IRS regulations) that option is not available. Then a paper version of the return must be sent to the IRS. Here is the list of these cases:

- Previous years returns
- Amended returns
- Dual-status alien tax returns
- Married filing separately with the non-resident spouse returns
- Selected state returns with the non-US mailing address (we will let you know if you state allows e-filing)
- Tax returns including forms 5471, 8891, 8621 or other informational returns

Please make sure to use the correct mailing address and submit your paper return to the IRS Service Center that handles returns of your type. Always check with http://www.irs.gov/file/article/0,,id=111453,00.html to find the correct address. If you file in response to an IRS notice, check with the agent handling your case before mailing your tax return.

Tax Refunds

Tax Refund for American Expats:
Most expats know that they have to file a US tax return. They see it as an unfair obligation bestowed upon them, with few discernible benefits gained. However – what many do not realize is that they are often eligible for a refund! This article will explain what kinds of credits are available to Americans living abroad and how you can actually **get a refund** from the US government.

This is probably one of the most pleasant parts of our job – informing a client that he or she is actually due a tax refund from the government, especially if this possibility was never even considered! Often times we find a refund opportunity for clients who have self-prepared or used less competent accountants in the past.

Two Types of Tax Credits:
- **Non-Refundable Credits:** A nonrefundable credit is a dollar-for-dollar reduction of the tax liability that can only reduce the tax liability to zero. You will not see these credits as a refund amount on your tax return. However, they are extremely valuable as an offset tool reducing an existing tax liability.
- **Refundable credits:** A refundable tax credit is a tax credit that can reduce your tax liability beyond zero. These credits are a pleasant (sometimes frightening) surprise for expats who did not pay any tax in the U.S. and discovered a 4-digit figure in the "Amount you overpaid" box at the bottom of form 1040. We believe this is fair: like other Americans, expats are required to file U.S. tax returns - hence, like other Americans, expats should qualify for tax credits.

Examples of the most common Non-Refundable Credits:
1. **Child and Dependent Care Credit:** This credit is based on a percentage of the amount actually paid for qualified care expenses. **The caveat:** you must have earned income to receive this credit. If your salary is fully excluded via the **Foreign Earned Income Exclusion** and you have tax due on dividends or interest, you will not be able to reduce tax through this credit.
2. **Education Credits:** Hope and Lifetime Learning credits. The good news: you can receive education credits even if you do not have earned income and reduce tax on other income. However, you will not get a refund if no tax is due.
3. **Child Tax Credit:** Credit for taxpayers with a qualifying child. The credit is limited to $1,000 per qualifying child and can only offset tax due.

Examples of the most common Refundable Credits:
1. **Additional Child Tax Credit** – has the same requirement that regular child tax credit. **The caveat:** If your salary is fully excluded through the foreign earned income exclusion, you will not receive the refund. Expert tax preparers (read: us) know how to adjust the amount of excluded income in order to keep the taxpayer below the taxable level while making him qualified for the additional child tax credit.
2. **Earned Income Credit** – refundable credit for low income families. **The caveat:** you must have lived in the U.S. for at least 6 months of the filing year to qualify for the credit.
3. **Adoption Credit** - refundable for adoptions finalized in 2010 or 2011

4. Excess Social Security Credit - If you work for more than one employer during the year, each U.S. employer is required to withhold social security taxes up to the maximum for that year. If you have withheld from your pay more than the annual maximum, you qualify for a refund.
5. **American Opportunity Credit** – Good news: a cash refund for qualified higher education expenses can now be paid directly to the students earning below the taxable level. **Caveat #1:** student cannot be listed as a dependent on parents' tax return. **Caveat #2:** graduate students do not qualify for this credit. The Tax Relief and Job Creation Act of 2010 extends the AOTC for two additional years until Dec. 31, 2012

The list of 8 types of credits listed above is not exhaustive. However – the larger point we'd like to make is twofold:

- It is possible to get a refund from the government as a US Expat living abroad.
- US Taxes are complicated – and much more so if the taxpayer is an expatriate. This is why we encourage expats to work with a qualified professional. Not only will you save yourself from making a costly mistake (and anguish of uncertainty), but also ensure that you're minimizing your tax liability - and possibly even getting a refund!

How Many Refunds Are Lost?
If you are actually due a tax refund, it's important that IRS has your correct details. Last year the agency released statement stating that they have over $150 million in undelivered refunds. Accounting today recently explained how the IRS found themselves in this situation in the article "IRS Stuck with $153.3 Million in Undelivered Returns." (http://www.accountingtoday.com/news/IRS-Undelivered-Tax-Refunds-60913-1.html?ET=webcpa:e1995:232069a:&st=email)
This is already becoming an annual occurrence:

"In what has turned into an annual ritual for the service, the IRS said it has a fortune waiting in its coffers that could not be delivered to taxpayers because of mailing address errors. Taxpayers can still claim their refunds, though, and can probably use a little help from their accountants. The average size of an undelivered refund check this year is $1,547."

How to Avoid Losing Your US Expat Tax Refund
IRS is encouraging taxpayers to take advantage of e-filing and electronic deposit options that are available to taxpayers around the globe. By avoiding the postal system, you reduce the likelihood that your refund will be lost.

"…taxpayers can put an end to lost, stolen or undelivered checks by choosing direct deposit when they file their tax returns, either on paper or electronically. Last year, more than 78.4 million taxpayers chose to receive their refund through direct deposit. Taxpayers can receive refunds directly through their bank account, split a tax refund into two or three financial accounts, or more recently buy a savings bond with the money.

Online Tax Payments

How to Remit Online Payment for Your US Expat Taxes
The deadline of June 15 for US expats has come and gone, and there are those who have still yet to pay their tax balance owed to the IRS. There still may be time for you to remit your payment online to avoid penalties being assessed. It's true that you could send a check, but the processing time of making a payment online is much more efficient and helps to guarantee your payment will be processed before negative action takes place. Here is a convenient list of links to help you satisfy your IRS tax debt online:

EFTPS (Electronic Federal Tax Payment System)
You must register online to take advantage of this option. After successful registration you are sent a letter which will help you complete your online payment. It generally takes around 10 business days to receive the letter after registering. Registration for EFTPS requires you to have an active checking account, but there is no fee assessed for online payments made.
Register at https://www.eftps.gov/eftps/

PAY1040
- This is a popular option for expats with a foreign bank account. Although there is a small charge applied for taking advantage of this option (generally under $4), payments can be made quickly and without having to register.
- To pay using this option, visit https://www.pay1040.com/

Official Payments
- This online payment venue typically charges 2.35% of the total amount paid and a minimum payment of $3.95. You may be able to take advantage of a flat fee of $3.95 if you pay using a Visa debit card.
- You may remit state, local, and educational payments.
- You have the option of paying by phone by calling 1-888-UPAY-TAX (1-888-872-9829).
- Visit https://www.officialpayments.com/fed for more information.

Pay USA Tax
- Besides EFTPS, this is the least expensive option. Pay USA Tax charges a flat fee of $3.49 for debit cards and 1.89% of payments made with major credit cards.
- Pay USA Tax accepts overseas payments by a variety of accepted cards (Accel, Discover,
- MasterCard, NYCE, Pulse, Star, and Visa)
- You may pay by phone at 1-888-9-PAY-TAX (1-888-972-9829).
- Use this payment option by visiting https://www.payusatax.com/.

Important Note
IRS tax payments should technically be remitted by the April deadline each tax year to avoid the extra cost of penalties and interest. This applies to all taxpayers (including US Citizens living abroad) – despite whether or not they qualify for the automatic filing extension of June 15. To get more information about late payments from the IRS, http://www.irs.gov/taxtopics/tc653.html

Alternative Minimum Tax

Many expats realize when they file their taxes that they don't owe quite as much as they thought they would. In order to protect abuse of the many available deductions and exclusions, the IRS has an Alternative Minimum Tax (AMT) in place. The IRS recently issued a series of important updates about AMT, and many of our overseas clients are affected by this information.

Before we delve into the AMT, let's take a brief look at its history. The Alternative Minimum Tax was first imposed by the IRS in 1969 to prevent high income taxpayers from avoiding tax liability altogether by claiming all of the deductions and exemptions possible. Although the AMT was originally enacted to target 155 high-income households, it now affects millions of families each year. The number of households that pay the tax has increased significantly in the last decade: In 1997, for example, 605,000 taxpayers paid the AMT; by 2008, the number of affected taxpayers jumped to 3.9 million, or about 4% of individual taxpayers. A total of 27% of households that paid the AMT in 2008 had adjusted gross income of $200,000 or less.

AMT is not adjusted with Inflation
While many aspects of IRS taxation are adjusted for inflation, the AMT is not. During certain times of economic fluctuation, middle class taxpayers may find they are subject to the AMT. Citizens who are at high risk of an imposition of AMT are expats, and this is due largely in part to the many deductions and exclusions available to expats.

Bush Tax Cuts & AMT for Americans Working Abroad
While many aspects of IRS taxation are adjusted for inflation, the AMT is not. During certain times of economic fluctuation, m

For what Exemptions am I Eligible under the Alternative Minimum Tax on my Expat Tax Return?
The IRS offers varied exemption rates for different filing statuses. In the event you are responsible for the AMT, you will be able to claim a certain amount of exemptions depending on your filing status. These statutes were last updated in 2010, and they are:

- $47,450 for singles and heads of household;
- $36,225 for a married person filing separately;
- $72,450 for a married couple filing a joint return and qualifying widows and widowers.

More Details on the Alternative Minimum Tax
Use the IRS AMT Assistant to determine whether you may be subject to the AMT. Taxpayers can find more information about the Alternative Minimum Tax and how it impacts them by accessing IRS Form 6251, Alternative Minimum Tax —Individuals, and its instructions at http://www.irs.gov or by calling 800-TAX-FORM (800-829-3676).

IRS Notices

If you receive the IRS Notice or Letter

DO NOT IGNORE IT! Like most other bad things, it will only get worse when ignored.

DO NOT PANIC. The IRS computers automatically generate notices and mail them without human interaction. Our experience is that tax notices are often inaccurate.

READ THE NOTICE CAREFULLY. Do not focus on threatening language and pay attention to the details instead: deadlines, required documents, and filing years.

FOCUS ON THE YEAR AND TAX FORM in question. It is easy to jump to conclusions, so make sure you understand which tax form and year (or quarter) is being addressed.

RESPOND BEFORE THE DEADLINE. Most notices have 30 days or 90 days to respond to it. If you are unsure you can handle it before the deadline, request additional time.

DO NOT GET ANGRY OR BLAME YOUR TAX PROFESSIONAL. The IRS has the authority from Congress to audit any taxpayer's last three tax returns. The IRS uses a complex statistical formula to try and identify where they can generate the most tax revenue, but they still use a random sample to keep everyone respectful of their civic duty to pay taxes.

DO NOT SEND MONEY until and unless you are sure you agree with the notice. People often pay tax they did not owe because they are intimidated by the IRS and want to 'get over with it'.

READ THE NOTICE AGAIN. Read the notice in detail, and try to find the reason they say you owe or what you did wrong. Highlight or underline the main points.

CONTACT THE PREPARER. If the tax return in question was prepared by a professional, make sure to contact the preparer and send (mail, fax or email) them a copy. They will help you determine one of three possibilities: 1) the IRS made the mistake or has incorrect information, 2) something was missed in the preparation, or 3) vital information was not provided to the preparer. If it was a preparation error, the preparer should be willing to handle the matter for you at no extra fee. If it was an IRS error, or an error in the information you provided, you will want to ask about fees before having your tax preparer handle it for you.

DOCUMENT COMMUNICATION Communicate before the deadline. Send letters via certified mail, and keep a copy for your records. If calling, make detailed notes of the conversation, including date; time, number called, and the name and ID number of the IRS agent.

REQUEST ADDITIONAL TIME. If you are getting close to the deadline stated in the notice, call for additional time. You can usually obtain an additional 60 days to respond to the notice if you will simply contact the IRS (before the deadline stated in the notice) by phone, fax, or letter that you need more time to gather facts and respond to the notice. If you call, document (see #10 above).

BE PATIENT. If the notice is incorrect you will have the burden of proving your side. So, be prepared for a lengthy process to get it straightened out. It can take months of phone calls and letters during which the IRS computers will continue sending out notices. Keep detailed notes of all phone calls, and keep copies of all letters sent and received.

PAYMENT If you understand the notice (and the cause of the additional tax) and you agree that you owe more taxes, then you can either pay the tax or request a payment plan (installment arrangement). Most notices have a place to sign if you agree with their assessment. If you return the signed assessment without full payment, they will send you a bill for the balance and Form 9465, Installment Agreement Request. Complete and submit the Installment Agreement Request if you cannot pay the balance due. Be sure to choose a monthly amount you can afford, since missing a payment will void your installment agreement.

REQUEST ABATEMENT OF PENALTIES. You may be able to receive an abatement of all or most of the penalties that have been assessed and disclosed in the notice. In general, taxes and interest are statutory and cannot be abated, but penalties can. I suggest that you pay only the tax portion of the notice (if you agree that you owe it) and include with your payment a written request for abatement of penalties along with a reason. The IRS is required to consider waiving penalties for reasonable cause.

IRS Penalties

If you owe taxes, the Internal Revenue Service will calculate penalties and interest on the amount owed. If you have a refund, the IRS may pay you interest on the delayed refund. (Note the difference between "will" and "may" - the IRS generally pays interest on refunds that have been delayed because of slow processing by the IRS. Since most late tax returns take longer to process, the IRS "may" pay you interest on based on the extra amount of time it takes them to process your return.) **If you have a refund, there is no penalty for filing late.** Penalties are calculated on the amount due. Since there is no amount due, there is no penalty.

If you have a balance due on a late tax return, the IRS will calculate additional penalties and interest. There are three separate penalties:

- Failure to File Penalty
- Failure to Pay Penalty
- Interest

Each is calculated differently. Let's take a look at each one.

Failure to File Penalty

The failure-to-file penalty is calculated based on the time from the deadline of your tax return (including extensions) to the date you actually filed your tax return. The penalty is **5% for each month the tax return is late, up to a total maximum penalty of 25%.** The percentage is of the tax due as shown on the tax return. If your tax return is more than five months late, simply multiply your balance due by 25% to calculate your failure to file penalty.

Failure to Pay Penalty

The failure-to-pay penalty is calculated based on the amount of tax you owe. **The penalty is 0.5% for each month the tax is not paid in full.** There is no maximum limit to the failure-to-pay penalty. The penalty is calculated from the original payment deadline (the original April 15th filing deadline) until the balance due is paid in full.

Interest

Interest is calculated based on how much tax you owe. Interest rates change every three months. Currently, the IRS interest rate for underpayment of tax is **4% per year**. The interest is calculated for each day your balance due is not paid in full.

. For the specific list of penalties that IRS can assess for failure to file specific forms, please see the following list.

Penalty for failing to file the Form TD F 90-22.1 (Report of Foreign Bank and Financial Accounts, commonly known as an "FBAR").

United States citizens, residents and certain other persons must annually report their direct or indirect financial interest in, or signature authority (or other authority that is comparable to signature authority) over, a financial account that is maintained with a financial institution located in a foreign country if, for any calendar year, the aggregate value of all foreign accounts exceeded $10,000 at any time during the year. Generally, the civil penalty for willfully failing to file an FBAR can be as high as the greater of $100,000 or 50 percent of the total balance of the foreign account per violation. See 31 U.S.C. § 5321(a)(5). Non-willful violations that the IRS determines were not due to reasonable cause are subject to a $10,000 penalty per violation.

- **A penalty for failing to file Form 3520, Annual Return to Report Transactions With Foreign Trusts and Receipt of Certain Foreign Gifts.** Taxpayers must also report various transactions involving foreign trusts, including creation of a foreign trust by a United States person, transfers of property from a United States person to a foreign trust and receipt of distributions from foreign trusts under IRC § 6048.This return also reports the receipt of gifts from foreign entities under section 6039F.The penalty for failing to file each one of these information returns, or for filing an incomplete return, is 35 percent of the gross reportable amount, except for returns reporting gifts, where the penalty is five percent of the gift per month, up to a maximum penalty of 25 percent of the gift.
- **A penalty for failing to file Form 3520-A, Information Return of Foreign Trust With a U.S. Owner.** Taxpayers must also report ownership interests in foreign trusts, by United States persons with various interests in and powers over those trusts under IRC § 6048(b).The penalty for failing to file each one of these information returns or for filing an incomplete return, is five percent of the gross value of trust assets determined to be owned by the United States person.
- **A penalty for failing to file Form 5471, Information Return of U.S. Persons with Respect to Certain Foreign Corporations.**
Certain United States persons who are officers, directors or shareholders in certain foreign corporations (including International Business Corporations) are required to report information under IRC §§ 6035, 6038 and 6046.The penalty for failing to file each one of these information returns is $10,000, with an additional $10,000 added for each month the failure continues beginning 90 days after the taxpayer is notified of the delinquency, up to a maximum of $50,000 per return.
- **A penalty for failing to file Form 5472,** Information Return of a 25% Foreign-Owned U.S. Corporation or a Foreign Corporation Engaged in a U.S. Trade or Business. Taxpayers may be required to report transactions between a 25 percent foreign-owned domestic corporation or a foreign corporation engaged in a trade or business in the United States and a related party as required by IRC §§ 6038A and 6038C. The penalty for failing to file each one of these information returns, or to keep certain records regarding reportable transactions, is $10,000, with an additional $10,000 added for each month the failure continues beginning 90 days after the taxpayer is notified of the delinquency.
- **A penalty for failing to file Form 926, Return by a U.S. Transferor of Property to a Foreign Corporation.** Taxpayers are required to report transfers of property to foreign corporations and other information under IRC § 6038B. The penalty for failing to file each one of these information returns is ten percent of the value of the property transferred, up to a maximum of $100,000 per return, with no limit if the failure to report the transfer was intentional.
- **A penalty for failing to file Form 8865, Return of U.S. Persons With Respect to Certain Foreign Partnerships.** United States persons with certain interests in foreign partnerships use this form to report interests in and transactions

of the foreign partnerships, transfers of property to the foreign partnerships, and acquisitions, dispositions and changes in foreign partnership interests under IRC §§ 6038, 6038B, and 6046A. Penalties include $10,000 for failure to file each return, with an additional $10,000 added for each month the failure continues beginning 90 days after the taxpayer is notified of the delinquency, up to a maximum of $50,000 per return, and ten percent of the value of any transferred property that is not reported, subject to a $100,000 limit.

- **Fraud penalties** imposed under IRC §§ 6651(f) or 6663. Where an underpayment of tax, or a failure to file a tax return, is due to fraud, the taxpayer is liable for penalties that, although calculated differently, essentially amount to 75 percent of the unpaid tax.
- **A penalty for failing to file a tax return** imposed under IRC § 6651(a)(1). Generally, taxpayers are required to file income tax returns. If a taxpayer fails to do so, a penalty of 5 percent of the balance due, plus an additional 5 percent for each month or fraction thereof during which the failure continues may be imposed. The penalty shall not exceed 25 percent.
- **A penalty for failing to pay the amount of tax shown on the return** under IRC § 6651(a)(2). If a taxpayer fails to pay the amount of tax shown on the return, he or she may be liable for a penalty of .5 percent of the amount of tax shown on the return, plus an additional .5 percent for each additional month or fraction thereof that the amount remains unpaid, not exceeding 25 percent.
- **An accuracy-related penalty on underpayments** imposed under IRC § 6662. Depending upon which component of the accuracy-related penalty is applicable, a taxpayer may be liable for a 20 percent or 40 percent penalty.
-

Amended Returns

Filing a US expat tax return can be challenging – especially if it's the first time you've had to file taxes as an American Expatriate. Because filing a US expat tax return is as complicated as it is, it's not uncommon for taxes to be filed incorrectly or incompletely. Income may have been forgotten, deductions may not have been taken, and the list goes on. In this article, we will take a deeper look at why an amended return is necessary and a few things you should know about filing such a return.

Why File an Amended Tax Return?
The broad answer to this question is: You should file an amended return if the information on your original US expat tax return is incorrect. It's possible that you will discover that you misfiled your taxes somehow on your own, and it's also possible that the IRS will notify you of your mistake and insist that you file an amended return. This, of course, is generally only in a situation in which the IRS would receive more money; they probably won't require you to file an amended return if you missed some of the deductions that are available to you.

So what are the reasons why you would need to file an amended return?
Missing Income
Perhaps you filed your US expat tax return and subsequently received a W-2 or 1099 in the mail that wasn't claimed on your taxes. Maybe you had self-employment income you forgot to report. Whatever the case may be, you should file an amended return so that all income is reported.

Missing Forms
There are a variety of schedules and forms required along with Form 1040. Different types of income are reported on these forms, and it's possible that you either didn't claim the income you were supposed to or you simply entered it into the wrong line on the wrong form.

Incorrect Information on Forms
This is a rather broad reason for needing to file an amendment US expat tax return, as it could be one of many things that are wrong with the form. Perhaps you claimed more dependents than you actually had or, conversely, failed to claim all of your dependents. It's also possible that you filed with the wrong status. These and other mistakes may affect the size of your return or the amount you owe to the IRS significantly.

Missing Deductions or Exclusions
American Expatriates have a wide variety of deductions and exclusions available to them to help minimize their US tax liability. It's possible that you just found out about certain exclusions or deductions you didn't even know existed when you filed your original US expat tax return. If you owed the IRS in previous years, you may be entitled to a refund after filing an amended return and claiming all the deductions and exclusions available to you.

Improperly Claimed Deductions or Exclusions
As easy as not knowing about deductions which are available to you is claiming deductions for which you don't actually qualify. Perhaps you heard about the FEIE (Foreign Earned Income Exclusion) (http://www.us-taxman.com/feie.php) but you were unaware of the

physical presence requirements of having lived in your host country. If you hadn't lived there for at least 330 days prior to your filing a return, you do not qualify for the deduction and would – therefore – need to file an amended return to correct your mistake.

Time Limit for Filing an Amended US Expat Tax Return
Whether you discovered your filing mistake on your own or you were notified by the IRS that you are required to file an amended return, it's best to get it done and over with as soon as possible. The more rapidly you correct the situation, the more additional fees and interest you can avoid. If you're expecting to receive a refund after you file your amended return, it must be within 3 years of having filed your original return. If you are amending a return older than 3 years, you will not receive a refund from the IRS.

How to File an Amended US Expat Tax Return
First things first: You cannot electronically file an amended return; paper returns for amending an original return are required. The form you need to file is Form 1040X, Amended US Individual Income Tax Return. You can find this form on the IRS website. If you are filing amended returns for multiple years, remember that you must file a different Form 1040X for each year. For easier processing, make sure to send each year's amended return in a separate envelope. If you received a letter from the IRS, make sure to send you return to the IRS Service Center outlined in the letter. If you did not receive a letter from the IRS, be sure to follow the instructions for Form 1040X and mail your amended return(s) to the indicated IRS Service Center.

Additional Details about Form 1040X
Make sure to clearly indicate the year for which you are filing an amended return at the top of Form 1040X by checking the appropriate box. Also, make sure to check the correct filing status for the corresponding tax year, even if it isn't changing.

To fill out Form 1040X, you will be required to fill out 3 columns next to each entry on the form. The first column will be the information on your original return. The second column will be the difference between the original and the amended amount, and the third column will be the actual amended amount. You will be required to provide all this information for every detail about income, deductions, and all other lines on the form.

There will be a section (Part III) on Form 1040X for you to state the reason of needing to file an amended US expat tax return. If you do not have enough room on the form for your explanation, you may attach an additional sheet outlining your reasons for having to file an amended tax return.

Conclusion
If you are a US Expatriate and your previous years' returns had significant balances owed to the IRS, it's possible that you failed to take some or all of the deductions and exclusions available to you. If you feel like you may receive a refund by filing an amended return with the IRS, make sure to contact a US Expat Tax Professional (http://www.us-taxman.com) to discuss your circumstances. If you've received a letter from the IRS informing you of a requirement to file an amended return and you need help filing Form 1040X, US Taxman can help.

IRS Audits

In the past, IRS rarely audited US Citizens who filed tax returns from abroad. This may, however, soon change due to a recently authorized increase in funding and staff in the IRS international tax department [http://www.ombwatch.org/node/10201 and http://www.journalofaccountancy.com/Web/20103170.htm].

We have been recently provided with the document used by the IRS to conduct audits of Form 2555, which is filed to claim the Foreign Earned Income Exclusion (http://www.us-taxman.com/feie.php) (FEIE). This audit is normally conducted by post and the IRS makes its decision based on the answers and supporting documents supplied by the taxpayer.

The following form is used by the IRS to audit expatriates claiming the FEIE. Download and examine it to determine if you have adequate support for your Form 2555 in case you become subject to an income tax audit by the IRS in the future.

If you find yourself subject to an IRS audit for any reason, let us know - we can help. We have helped many taxpayers (including expatriates) before the IRS on audits involving numerous issues in the Tax Code and have an excellent track record of success for our clients.

Audits are a Fact of Life

So you've been targeted for an audit by the IRS...The most important thing for you to remember is: It's not worth losing any sleep over! The IRS simply wants to conduct verification on the items you've claimed. As you may remember, IRS did not request any supporting documents with your Tax Return (that's why we mostly rely on our own Questionnaire when preparing your return). The purpose of the audit is to verify that the information supplied is correct.

Most audits performed are done so without any changes being made to your original tax return; as most of the people who file are able to back up every item listed. The most important step you can take once you are notified of an audit is to begin compiling all of your paperwork on which you relied to file your taxes in the first place. Also, don't forget to stay calm and abstain from becoming defensive. If you need professional assistance, do not wait!

Why Am I Being Audited?

When you first receive notification of an audit, your first question is most likely, "Why am I being audited?!" Before we get into the possibilities of 'why,' let's first examine the list of 'why nots.' It's NOT because you forgot to pay a parking ticket before moving overseas or anything to do with any of the decisions you've made not related to your taxes. It all likelihood, you could have been just a random return which was chosen to conduct an audit for no reason other than to conduct an audit. Some more concrete reasons may include any of the following:

- Calculation errors
- Incomplete return (lacking required schedules)
- Failing to report all income from 1099 or W-2 Forms

- Setting off one of the many 'secret alarms' which vary each year. The most common alarms for the IRS may include abnormally high charitable donations; excessive credits or exclusions; excessive travel, meals, and entertainment; and more.

Even though it may be an interesting guessing game, odds are you will not figure out exactly why you are being audited. The more important investment of your energies, however, should be what to do next to make this as stress free as possible.

What to Expect?

Once your tax return has been selected for an audit, you will receive correspondence by mail at the address listed on your most current US tax return. If your current address is in an overseas location, the IRS will conduct the audit via total mail correspondence. More times than not, the IRS generally only targets 1 year and chooses one form to audit. For example, if you submitted a schedule A among other forms, the IRS may only be interested in auditing the items listed on your Schedule A. If you have no special additional forms you may find that your entire 1040 is examined.

Upon receiving your notice, you are going to want to ask yourself honestly, "Can I handle this on my own?" If you filed your tax return yourself and you have a complete understanding of each item on your return you should be able to make it through an audit without any trouble. If, however, you hired a professional to prepare your taxes and you're confused about the claims within them, you will most likely want to hire an expert to help you with compilation of documentation and communicate with the IRS through your audit.

Whether you seek advice from a professional or you decide to communicate with the IRS yourself, here are a few important tips to consider:

- Organize all your documentation well. Organize each section of your return you will need by category rather than by date.
- Don't forget that the IRS representative is sworn to the US government. Yes, they are people just like you; but they do not need information which could put them in a tough position with their sworn duties.
- Be respectful to and honest with the auditor. Try not to get defensive, and remain calm.
- Only provide information which is being requested – nothing more.

The entire process of an audit could very well take months, and audits conducted by correspondence have a tendency to take much longer. Al finale, you will sent a notice in the mail regarding the final outcome of your audit. If lady luck is in your favor, you will be notified of a refund which is due to you. If you are moderately lucky there will be no changes made to your return at all. If luck is not on your side at all, you will be notified of a balance due to the IRS. If you disagree with the decision you will be able to appeal, but we will touch more on that later.

If you are informed of a balance due and you do not wish to appeal, the best thing you can do is to pay the balance as soon as possible and be done with the entire thing. If you are unable to pay the balance and are interested in setting up a payment plan with the IRS, contact a representative immediately. Failure to communicate with the IRS could result in hefty penalties and interest which is applied daily.

What Sort Of Documentation Will I Need?

When compiling documentation to share with your assigned auditor, you will be selecting documents which prove the claims you've made on your US tax return. For example, sticking with the previous instance of a Schedule A being audited, you would compile your medical and dental receipts, all receipts you saved to prove your local tax deduction, mortgage interest, charitable donation receipts, and all job related receipts which were not reimbursed by your employer. If – for whatever reason – you do not have all the receipts, you can back up your claims with bank or credit card statements.

Can They Review Other Tax Years?

Yes. Remember one of the tips above during all of your conversations with the auditor: Only provide answers to that which is asked – nothing more. If an auditor finds something suspicious in a return, they have the right (and generally enact the right) to investigate further – even if it has nothing to do with their original agenda. This rule does not only apply to the current tax year or even taxpayer; the only limit to the lengths a full investigation can go is that of tax returns which are 3 years or older.

What Happens if I Disagree With the Results?

If the audit has unfavorable results, and you disagree with the outcome you have an opportunity to fight it. Before enlisting any of your options, you should conduct your own research by reading over the IRS publications (http://www.us-taxman.com/taxpublications.php) and documents in order to make sure you have a leg to stand on with proof of your claims. Cite the IRS code directly and support it with the documentation you have. You generally have 30-60 days to appeal the decision of the IRS. You may be able to resolve the issue within 30 days without having to file a formal appeal. Many clients find they are able to get an IRS supervisor or director to see things their way. IRS directors are human beings, and they are able to view things logically. They know that both the IRS and citizens make mistakes, and they are as open to your being right as they are to your being wrong. They want to settle if at all possible before your case reaches the level of formal appeal.

If you are unable to reason with a supervisor you can submit a formal appeal. Before doing this, it is highly recommended that you seek the advice of a tax professional or tax attorney to help you better fight your case.

Conclusion

It is possible for an audit to be free of stress. Planning ahead and being prepared are 2 very key components to a stress-free audit. When you file your taxes, assume you will be audited and keep all of your documentation in a safe place. Keep this documentation for at least 3 years, and remember to enlist the help of a tax professional when you need guidance.

The IRS Long arm

We are frequently asked by expatriates living and working outside of the United States if the IRS would ever be able to discover that their annual US expat tax returns are not filed. The simple answer to this question is: **Yes, the IRS will be able to track you down if you are not filing your US expat tax return annually.**

Now we will get into the ways in which the IRS will be able to identify you as a delinquent taxpayer and hold you accountable for your tax liability:

- You apply for Social Security or pension benefits;
- You open a US based financial account;
- You inherit money or assets from parents, grandparents, or others who have passed on;
- You are reported by a whistle-blower; the IRS offers 'finder fees' for individuals who report other individuals for not paying their income taxes. The highest known whistle-blower fee so far is $104M;
- You renew your passport and are forced to provide your social security number which is, then, sent to the IRS;
- Your foreign income or financial accounts are reported to the IRS due to an information sharing treaty enacted by FATCA;
- You register on the internet in a public domain such as Facebook or Twitter;
- You register the birth of a child born overseas with the US Embassy in your host country;
- You are involved in a marriage, divorce, or some other matter of public record;
- You enter the United States using a foreign passport which indicates that you were born in the US;
- Your name appears on stolen information on foreign financial accounts which are passed on to the IRS;
- Your adult children submit applications to universities or other learning institutions in the United States and provide information about income and payments;
- You are listed on another's US expat tax return or foreign business documents which have been shared with the IRS;
- You are indicated on suspicious activity forms submitted to the IRS (this form is often submitted by banks, auto dealers, and other institutions which have reason to suspect tax evasion and other suspicious activities);
- You are included in information which has been provided to SOCA (Serious Organized Crimes Office) or the United States Treasury Financial Crimes Enforcement Network;
- You are identified via information provided to the IRS or Department of Treasury by an individual taking advantage of an OVDI (Offshore Voluntary Disclosure Initiative) http://www.us-taxman.com/disclosure.php
- Or you are a member involved in forming a corporation or partnership in a foreign country which requires you to identify your ownership as an American Citizen.

The number of countries which share information about US Citizens with the IRS is steadily ncreasing. Information sharing treaties are helping more countries (not only the United States) to realize more tax revenue than ever before, and the internet is making it more convenient to share information and track down individuals who are not filing regular US expat tax returns with the IRS or reporting foreign financial accounts to the Department of Treasury.

If you have been delinquent with your US expat tax returns to the IRS or have failed to report your foreign bank accounts in excess of $10K to the Department of Treasury and you need help filing back taxes or taking advantage of the 2012 OVDI while it is still in effect, make sure to get in touch with a US expat tax professional (http://www.us-taxman.com) who can help you resolve your tax issues with as little repercussions as possible.

Expatriate Tax Situation Analyzed

How do you begin to analyze the impact renunciation would have on your taxes?

We've put together some general considerations that can help you analyze your situation. Everyone's situation is clearly different, but these are what we'd consider useful starting points. Some are obvious, others not so.

You can jump straight to a section by clicking on a link below, or just scroll down through the page to read them one after another.

- Hoping the system will change isn't the answer. Neither is dropping off the radar.
- Do you need a tax professional?
- How much time you can spend in the U.S. after expatriation and still be taxed as a non-resident
- Figuring if the U.S. burden increases your total tax on earned income
- Investment income
- Future changes in your life
- Retirement, savings, and tax
- Changes in tax codes
- Inheritance issues: spouse and/or heir(s) not U.S. citizen(s)
- Inheritance issues: spouse and/or heir(s) U.S. citizen(s)
- Inheritance issues: receiving an inheritance from a U.S. citizen
- Considering the "deemed sale" of the exit tax

Hoping the system will change isn't the answer. Neither is dropping off the radar.

We estimate the probability that the U.S. will switch to a purely residency-based tax system is zero.

Despite the hopes of many people who find themselves forced to consider expatriating, the reality is that U.S. citizenship-based taxation is not going to change. If anything, the tax burden for overseas citizens will most likely only increase, along with the reporting requirements, restrictions, and regulations.

There is no reason for Congress to ever surrender the tax revenue from citizens abroad. Overseas citizens are an extremely convenient target: they have little political power, they generally don't vote (and even when they do, their votes are not aggregated in one district/state but are instead scattered around the country), and they can be easily caricatured as rich tycoons sipping pia-coladas on the beach.

Simply ignoring their U.S. tax obligation has worked for many people until now, but international information-sharing, more effective tracking systems and massively increasing IRS resources devoted to overseas compliance are combining to make it much more difficult to successfully "disappear off the radar".

For us, the bottom line is: if you want to keep your citizenship, then you have to pay taxes and comply with all the regulations. If not, you should renounce.

Do you need a tax professional?

We don't believe that the issues are so complex that normal people can't understand them and calculate their own tax scenarios. This isn't an esoteric branch of physics that only a miniscule portion of the population can fathom. Even the most difficult technical details in the world of tax aren't computationally or intellectually so difficult; it just means that you have to read lots of regulations and figure out how to put them together. Boring, yes; needlessly complicated, yes... but truly difficult, no.

If you navigated to this site and are reading this, then we'd bet that you have the ability to understand all the tax issues. Good summaries and explanations about expatriation are hard to find on the internet, but the codes and laws themselves are available online. Finding the information can be difficult at times, but the list of resources we put together here will help you get started and save you enormous amounts of time.

Also, it's important to realize that you're probably affected by only a limited number of tax regulations. Tax codes in many countries - and especially in the U.S. - are huge, but fortunately the parts relevant to any one person are fairly manageable. Each person has their individual items that need to be researched, but very few people have such a wide variety of income and assets that they need to deal with so many different issues.

We feel that by investigating and understanding all the tax regulations yourself, you'll do yourself a favor in the long run. No one knows your situation better than you, and no one cares about it more than you, so if you learn the information yourself, you'll be the one who can do the best job for yourself.

On the other hand, learning about tax means you have to spend enormous amounts of time to research all the details, all the most-recent changes, all the subtleties of the ways different tax regulations interact with each other. And your time is important; it could be a lot more valuable to spend that time doing something else more productive or enjoyable.

Also, when dealing with renunciation tax law specifically, and international tax law in general, there are lots of gray areas that are not clear. Issues that we've come across that are especially confusing when considering U.S. expatriation are: inheritance/estate tax, particularly if you have property in U.S. at the time of death; tax on trusts; tax on a business you own with operations in several countries.

And the interaction of U.S. tax law with the tax law of your country of residence could be particularly tricky. No tax law addresses every situation, and even the best explanations from the tax agencies cannot answer every specific situation that you could find yourself in. It can be helpful to have the guidance of someone who has been through it before; he won't be smarter than you or have greater ability, but his previous experience could save you time and (possibly) money. And if your tax issues are particularly varied or unusual, he might be able to draw for help on the specialized knowledge of a network of colleagues.

So if you don't want to make the huge time investment to run through the scenarios or you don't feel comfortable navigating through murky international tax regulations on your own, then work with a tax professional. Depending where you live, you might need to work with more than one person, because you'll be dealing with the tax code of the U.S. plus your country (is). In most major countries, though, there are tax pros who specialize in U.S. expatriate's tax, so one pro might be enough.

If you decide to work with a tax pro, our recommendation is to learn as much as you can on your own before meeting.

Your knowledge will help you make better use of the tax pro's skills and experience. The advantage of working with a professional is the previous experience and knowledge that he brings to your case, so your research will also help you to test him on it beforehand to see what he knows. The reality is that the field of expatriate tax seems to attract a lot of under-qualified types, and it's silly to pay him if he's learning on the job and on your time. Prepare a list of detailed questions about the tax law of the U.S. and your country of residence, about the existing tax treaties, and about the tax effects of U.S. expatriation on both your U.S. taxes and your non-U.S. taxes. The tax information on this site is fairly basic but should give you a good starting point for your questions. Any tax professional should know significantly more about these issues than what's on this site; if he doesn't, our opinion is that he's not worth your time or money.

How much time you can spend in the U.S. after expatriation and still be taxed as a non-resident

After expatriation, you will be treated as any other citizen of your country is treated. If your citizenship is from a visa-waiver country, you don't need a visa for visits up to 90 days. If your country is not on the visa-waiver list, you will need to apply for a visa, but barring any unusual circumstances, you will most likely be approved. (See here for our discussion of your legal rights after expatriation).

Regarding U.S. taxes, you will be treated as any other citizen of your country in almost all respects. Assuming you live outside the U.S. and don't have a green card, you will be taxed as a non-resident non-citizen on any U.S. source earnings, allowing you to benefit from no taxes on interest and capital gains.

However, you will be treated as resident for tax purposes if you spend enough time in the U.S. (including U.S. territorial waters) to meet the "substantial physical presence" test, defined as spending:

- At least 31 days in the current year
  AND
- At least 183 days during the 3 year period that includes the current year and the previous 2 years, where you count all of the days you spend in the U.S. in the current year, 1/3 of the days you spent in the previous year, and 1/6 of the days you spent in the second year before the current year.

In essence, under the "substantial physical presence test", you can spend an average of up to 4 months each year in the U.S. and not be resident for tax purposes.

Note that because of the different weights used to count days in each year, there are several permutations of time spent in the U.S. that are possible. For example, you could spend 180 days in year 1, 120 days in year 2, and 110 days in year 3, and still not be considered resident in any of those years.

Figuring if the U.S. burden increases your total tax on earned income

With the exception of the U.S., all countries in the world tax based on residency. So when thinking about the tax impact of renouncing U.S. citizenship, the tax system(s) of your current and future country(ies) of residence is obviously very important.

As a U.S. citizen, you're subject to taxes on your foreign earnings, but you're allowed to take a credit for (most) taxes paid to a foreign government. Assuming you live outside the U.S., you're also allowed to exclude the first $95,100 (as of 2012) in earned income from U.S. taxes.

So the total tax you pay to all countries on earned income (i.e., income from work as opposed to income from investments) will depend on how much you make and what tax rate your country of residence imposes. How the total tax on your earnings would be affected by renunciation of U.S. citizenship will depend on this combination.

In considering how renunciation will affect the total tax you pay on earnings, you have to evaluate both the tax rates in your country of residence relative to U.S. rates, and your earned income relative to the U.S. foreign earned income exclusion.

So what's this mean in practice? The devil is in the details, but we can make some generalizations:

If you live in a country with higher tax rates than the U.S., your total taxes are probably not higher because of the U.S. tax burden.

And even if your country of residence has lower taxes than the U.S. but your income is lower than $92,900, then the total taxes on your earned income probably isn't higher due to the U.S. obligation.

But if you live in a country with lower taxes than the U.S. and your earnings income is above the $95,100 limit, the total tax on your earned income is probably higher because of the U.S. tax burden.

Note that these are very big generalizations, and the details can sometimes dramatically change the conclusion. For example, definitions of income categories and types of taxes often do not match between the U.S. and other countries. In these situations, you could end up paying the higher of both rates in all situations AND be double-taxed in situations where the U.S. does not consider the foreign tax you pay to be creditable. We've seen some pretty unappealing results in specific cases, so it's definitely worth looking into the details of the interaction of U.S. tax law with that of your country of residence.

The way you earn your income is also important to consider when analyzing renunciation: If capital investment is an important part of producing your income, no more than 30% of your income can be counted as earned income and benefit from the exclusion. The rest is treated as investment income and fully taxed by the U.S.

This can have a dramatic effect for many individuals who are self-employed, invest their own money professionally, own and operate a business in which they invested money, have stakes in partnerships, etc. In essence, 70% of the income you earn from these activities is considered investment income and cannot be excluded; regardless of how much time you spend doing your activity. Many U.S. citizens working overseas are trapped by this and are subject to full taxation by both their country of residence and by the U.S.

Renunciation in these situations will very likely reduce your total tax burden.

Investment income
The U.S. foreign earned income exclusion of $95,100 (as of 2012) applies only to earnings from wages. It can't be applied to any money you earn from your own investments: not interest, not capital gains, not dividends. As a citizen, you're fully subject to taxes on all your investment income worldwide.

Depending on your situation, this can have a significant effect on your total tax burden. Take the example of a retired man living in a country that does not tax investment income. With no wage earnings, he doesn't qualify for the foreign earned income exclusion, and he is fully taxed by the U.S. for all his earnings. If he were to renounce U.S. citizenship, his total tax burden would be zero.

Another consideration is whether you make numerous investments in the U.S. In particular, whether you will in the future make numerous investments in the U.S. As we discussed here, the U.S. is a tax haven for non-resident non-citizen investors: most interest and capital gains are not taxed. If you expatriate, you will enjoy these tax-free investments as well.

[Remember that depending on your situation, you might have to pay the mark-to-market exit tax on the unrealized gain on all your assets at renunciation. But you have to meet the economic threshold tests, and even if you do, you still have an exclusion of $627,000 (as of 2010), so it's possible that you might have to pay nothing. See here for details.]

Future changes in your life
To complicate matters more, you have to think about the future.

Renunciation is not just for a year or two; it's a final, irrevocable lifetime decision. So as you consider the tax impact of renunciation, you have to think about the future of both your financial situation and the tax codes of different countries.

Think about your income. How will your earnings change? How will the ratio between your wage earnings and investment earnings change? When will you retire, and how will that affect your financial profile? All these issues could affect the tax impact of renunciation.

Think about where you'll live. If you plan to live and work in only one country for the rest of your life, then you only have to consider that country's tax system relative to the U.S. But if you move often between countries, or if you think you might ever move countries, then it's worth considering both the current and possible future rates in different places. Tax codes vary enormously and countries compete with their rates, so you can always find countries with systems which are more advantageous for you, but few people make their decision of where to live based solely on tax. Planning far into the future is difficult, but even your best guess can help guide you in your analysis.

Retirement, savings, and tax

Retirement is a major factor in analyzing the effect of renunciation.

Imagine that after retirement, you live primarily on the income from your investments, savings and pension/retirement receipts. As you will not be able to exclude any of this income from your U.S. taxes, you will be fully taxed by the U.S. on all your income. If you will retire in a country that has similar or higher tax rates than the U.S., it might make little difference. But if you plan to retire in a country with lower or no taxes, then your annual taxes would be significantly lower if you expatriate.

On the other hand, if you qualify as a "deemed expatriate" under the exit tax rules, and you have more than $627,000 (as of 2010) in unrealized profits, then you will have to pay the mark-to-market expatriation tax and any savings from lower future annual taxes might be negated. It all depends on your individual circumstances.

It's also important to consider that even many high-tax countries do not tax investment income, earnings from savings or capital gains. Belgium and New Zealand, for example, have marginal tax rates for earned income that are generally higher than the U.S., but have no capital gains taxes at all. If you live in such a country, and capital appreciation is or will be a a major source of your income, then expatriation could significantly lower your taxes.

The interplay of different tax regimes on retirement distributions could also affect your decision about renunciation. Payments from any private pension funds or retirement plans are fully taxed by the U.S.: they're considered investment income and can't be shielded with the foreign earned income exclusion.

An additional complication is that any benefits you may be entitled to from U.S. Social Security will be reduced by any payments you get from a foreign public retirement plan. Renunciation of citizenship would eliminate the U.S. tax obligation and reduce your taxes in most of these cases.

Additionally, although foreign taxes you pay on your pension receipts can often be used as a credit in calculating your U.S. taxes, there are still quite a few taxes you might have to pay in your country of residence which is not creditable. The result is guaranteed double taxation. There have proposals to correct this situation, but reducing revenue in order to benefit retired Americans overseas has not been a Congressional priority. Renunciation of citizenship in these cases would eliminate the double taxation.

Another issue to consider is where you invest. Many countries have high taxes on domestic investments, but do not tax investments abroad. As it's increasingly common to live in one country and invest in others, this can have a big impact on your after-tax income. As an example, if you live in such a country but all your investments are made in other countries, then you would not have to pay any tax where you reside. Nonetheless, as a U.S. citizen, you would be liable for U.S. taxes on your income despite the favorable tax laws of your country of residence. In this case, expatriation could significantly lower your taxes.

Finally, it's important to note that while residing overseas, you will not benefit from Medicare, regardless of how much you have contributed to it in the past.

Medicare benefits, the federal health insurance program for people 65 and over or disabled, are limited to the U.S. Note that this is regardless of whether you have or do not have U.S. citizenship.

Citizens overseas generally receive no benefits outside the U.S. from the program. Part A coverage is free but services can only be provided within the U.S. For Part B coverage, you have to pay a monthly premium, but even if you're paying the premium, the services are limited to within the U.S. Part D coverage, the prescription-drug benefit, is also limited to within the U.S. Groups representing retired Americans overseas have lobbied extensively for years to allow Medicare benefits for citizens abroad, but to date Congress has never acted.

Note that renunciation does not affect your eligibility for Social Security and Medicare. You are still eligible for full benefits of both after your renunciation. [As noted above, Medicare does not cover outside the U.S., so you'd have to travel to the U.S. to receive Medicare services, but this is the same for a citizen as for someone who's renounced].

Changes in tax codes

When considering renunciation, you'll also have to think about possible changes in tax codes in the future, both in the U.S. and in your country (ies) of residency. We realize that predicting tax code changes is like reading tea leaves, but because renunciation is for the rest of your life, you unfortunately have to at least try to make a stab at future trends.

Regarding the U.S. tax system, it's worth considering that benefits for U.S.-citizens abroad are constantly being eroded.

A large change in 2006 already hurt overseas taxpayers, and the trend seems to be even for even reduced benefits. Despite the hopes of Americans overseas groups, it appears very unlikely that the foreign earned income exclusion will be made unlimited, i.e. allow you to exclude all income earned overseas from your U.S. taxes. A bill was introduced by Senator DeMint (Rep., S.C.) and Rep. Meeks (Dem., N.Y.) to this effect in 2007, but got no support and died; the same legislation was introduced in 2009 (only by Rep. Meeks this time), and has similarly gotten nowhere.

On the other hand, the calls in Congress to reduce or even eliminate the foreign earned income exclusion are particularly noteworthy. In 2003, legislation to eliminate the exclusion - and thereby subject all income earned overseas to U.S. tax - was not only proposed, but actually was passed by the U.S. House as a way to partially fund an unrelated tax cut bill. Last minute maneuvering removed the elimination of the exclusion from the bill that was sent to the White House and which became law. Although the many lawmakers opposed to any exclusion for foreign income did not succeed in eliminating it, they did later manage to add to the TIPRA law (passed in 2005, effective in 2006) provisions which significantly reduced the tax benefits received by U.S. overseas citizens (see here for full discussion of how it worsened for overseas citizens).

We think it quite likely that the trend will continue: tax benefits given to U.S. citizens overseas will continue to be reduced or eliminated outright.

What tax law changes do you think are likely in the U.S.?

Another very obvious change that could impact many U.S.-citizens living outside the U.S. is the burden of ever-increasing reporting requirements. Reports of foreign accounts, calculations of paper profits from foreign exchange gains, tax years that do not match, etc: if you do taxes for the U.S. and another country, you know what a time-consuming and expensive hassle all the paperwork already can be.

The reporting burden of U.S.-citizens overseas has already increased over the last few years, and all signs from the U.S. government are that it will significantly increase even more over the next 2-3 years.

This is a real cost. We know of several families who own small businesses for whom the administrative burden of dealing with the IRS in addition to the tax authorities of where they reside was one of the factors which contributed to their renunciation.

In addition to changes in U.S. tax law, you also have to consider where you live. What changes are likely in your country(ies) of residence?

Inheritance issues: spouse and/or heir(s) not U.S. citizen(s)

If your spouse is not a U.S. citizen at the time of your death and if your assets are held outside the U.S., then it is clearly financially advantageous to have expatriated.

In fact, this is one of the bigger reasons behind several expatriations which we know of. As a U.S. citizen, you cannot transfer property tax-free to your non-U.S. spouse. There have been numerous complaints about this made by affected individuals, but we see no chance that this rule will ever change. Transfers to a citizen-spouse are allowed tax-free because the U.S. considers that it will eventually get a chance to tax the assets (presumably, when the citizen-spouse sells the assets or dies). But transfers to a non-citizen spouse effectively put the assets permanently out of the reach of U.S. taxation, so the U.S. wants to tax them before they "escape".

In contrast, as a non-U.S. citizen, your assets outside the U.S. will not be subject to U.S. estate taxes, and your spouse will not face any gift taxes. Note that this advantage doesn't depend on what your non-U.S. nationality is or where you live; as far as we know, there is no permutation of possible residency and citizenships worldwide where it would be better to have not renounced U.S. citizenship in this situation (if anyone does know of an example, please let us know).

For the same reasons, it's also similarly advantageous to have expatriated if your heir(s) is/are non-U.S. citizens.

Inheritance issues: spouse and/or heir(s) U.S. citizen(s)

The situation is more complicated if your spouse is a U.S. citizen. Note that we assume here that you live outside the U.S.

If you are a U.S. citizen, you may transfer unlimited property to your U.S.-citizen spouse upon your death free of U.S. taxes.

If you renounce citizenship, then as a non-resident non-U.S. citizen, you should still be able to transfer property free of U.S. estate taxes upon death to your U.S.-citizen spouse. However, due to the 2008 exit tax law, your spouse will have to pay a 35% tax on everything received from you above the gift exemption limit (currently $13,000) because you renounced U.S. citizenship.

If you and your spouse were to both renounce U.S. citizenship, then you would be able to pass him/her unlimited non-U.S. assets at any time free of all U.S. taxes.

U.S.-based assets, including U.S. stocks and U.S. real estate, are a different story.

The U.S. assets of non-resident non-citizens are subject to the U.S. estate tax and only the first $60,000 (as of 2009) is exempt. If you have renounced and then pass these U.S. assets to a U.S.-citizen spouse, you avoid the estate tax because you're allowed unlimited transfers to your U.S.-citizen spouse. However, your spouse will presumably have to pay the tax dictated by the gift-tax provision of the exit tax. (This issue is still murky, and no IRS guidelines have clearly said what happens in this situation. We assume the worst; as in most things related to tax, it's the safest bet).

If you give your U.S.-assets to anyone other than a U.S.-citizen spouse, then he/she will face the U.S. estate tax (although if the recipient is a U.S. citizen, he/she is exempted from paying the gift tax due to the fact that your estate already has paid an estate tax). Many expatriates aren't affected by this provision because they have few assets in the U.S., but if you do, we recommend investigating in detail because the issue is still unclear and could vary significantly based on your individual circumstances.

Be sure to confirm your residency status, because U.S. residency status for estate tax is figured differently than for income tax. For example, you could be a resident alien for income tax, but a non-resident for estate tax.

Inheritance issues: receiving an inheritance from a U.S. citizen

There's a different point to consider if you are a U.S. citizen and expecting an inheritance from another U.S. citizen. Under current U.S. law, inherited assets will step up their basis; in other words, the market price of the assets when you receive them in the inheritance will be considered to be your cost.

Thus, if you are considering expatriation, you have incentive to wait until immediately after receiving the inheritance to renounce citizenship. The estate will be taxed at the estate tax rate, but will benefit from the $5 million (as of 2011) exemption. At your expatriation, your net gain will be zero and you will pay no tax under the deemed sale. Note that the status of this step up in basis is tied to estate tax rules which could potentially expire and change based on the U.S. political situation at the end of 2012.

Considering the "deemed sale" of the exit tax

The exit tax imposed by the 2008 HEART act can be a very significant burden to expatriation for many. On the other hand, the advantage is that the law now allows you to make a clean break from U.S. taxation. In contrast to the previous system, you no longer have tax payments, U.S. tax planning, tax forms, U.S. source income definitions, and reporting requirements for the 10 years after your expatriation.

If your net worth is under $2 million and your average tax liability for the 5 years prior to your expatriation is under $145,000, then the exit tax doesn't apply to you and you can simply ignore it. Your tax obligations end on the day you expatriate. [To be precise, you still have to file Form 8854 to the IRS, but only to certify that the tax does not apply to you].

Or if you received dual citizenship of the U.S. and some other country at birth, if you continue to have the citizenship of that country, if you are taxed as a resident of that country, AND if you have been a resident of the U.S. for no more than 10 of the 15 years prior to renouncing U.S. citizenship, then you're also exempted from the exit tax, regardless of your net worth or level of income tax payments.

But if the exit tax applies to you, it could significantly affect your analysis. Some issues to consider:

The timing of your expatriation can be very important. Your assets will be valued as if they were sold on the day before your renunciation, so the prices on that day will determine the tax you pay.

For very illiquid assets, the exact day might make little difference. But for liquid assets such as stocks or commodity holdings or even certain real estate, there's enough daily volatility that your valuation - and thereby, the tax - might vary by several percent from one week to the next.

A major point to also consider if you have assets denominated in non-dollar currencies is the exchange rate. Your U.S. taxes will be based on the unrealized dollar gain. Given the dollar weakness over the last few years (last decade, actually), it's quite common that assets you own haven't appreciated much in value in the local currency, but show a gain of 20-50% when calculated in U.S. dollars.

You will be liable for tax on the dollar gain, even if the asset value hasn't moved in local currency.

In practice, this means you have to use both the exchange rate now and the exchange rate at the time of purchase in your calculations. You convert the purchase price into dollars at the then-prevailing exchange rate; convert the "deemed sale" price into dollars at the exchange rate of the day before your expatriation, then compare the difference to get your net gain or loss.

It can be a ridiculously complex task, particularly if you have many non-dollar assets purchased at different times. And given the steady weakness in the dollar over the last few years, the effect of this tax-code provision is quite likely to create phantom gains on which you will have to pay what are, unfortunately, very real taxes. As illogical as it is, this rule has been firmly settled for over a decade since a taxpayer challenged it up to the Court of Appeals and lost decisively. Even the Court acknowledged as "fair and reasonable" the taxpayer's argument that he had not realized any profit from dollar weakness, but ruled that a U.S. citizen must nonetheless use the U.S. dollar as his "functional currency" for all tax calculations (Quijano vs. United States, 1996). [If you used a local-currency mortgage to pay for a home, you could be particularly hard hit, as the taxpayer in that case was, by currencies moves in both directions: dollar weakness creates phantom dollar-gains on your house, which are taxable as capital gains, while dollar strength creates phantom dollar-gains on your mortgage, which are taxable as ordinary income].

For more discussion of taxes on these phantom gains you never receive and whether the absurdity will ever stop, see our discussion here.

[Note that it's possible that tax planning far enough in advance to create a qualified business unit (QBU) could partially mitigate this effect, but it can be difficult to meet the requirements. Moreover, it's very unclear if and how the exit tax would interact with the QBU. As of this writing, we have to assume that there would be no benefit].

Note that all these rules apply to any U.S. citizen: all citizens have to calculate their gains in dollars and pay taxes on the dollar income, even if it's a phantom gain that gave you no benefit. The only difference caused by renunciation is that as a covered expatriate, you must actually calculate and pay taxes as if you sold all your assets the day before renunciation. As a citizen, you pay the taxes when you actually do sell the assets.

If you are not covered by the exit tax (i.e., you're not a "covered expatriate", as described here), then renunciation effectively frees you from the tax burden caused by these foreign currency problems.

It's important to note that just as timing matters in the price of the asset, timing also matters in the exchange rate. You'll use the exchange rate on the day before your expatriation to calculate the dollar value of your assets. Exchange rates moves of 5-10% within a month are not unusual in the last few years for even the major currencies; this has a direct 1-to-1 impact on the valuation of your assets in dollars.

An obvious point is that you can't predict the movement of exchange rates, stocks, etc, so any day is as good as the next. This is clearly true. However, certain periods can be particularly advantageous. For example, we know several people who took advantage of the combination of low stock prices and rapid dollar appreciation in January-March 2009 to expatriate. Although they didn't know at the time how prices would move in the future, they did know that the unrealized dollar gains on their assets had dropped substantially when compared to just several months prior. In one case we know, the individual's unrealized gains in September 2008 would have been $1 million. Because of stock and dollar moves, his gains were slightly less than half that when calculated at his expatriation in March, 2009. The reduced net worth calculation put him under the $626,000 exemption and left him free from tax liability.

A different option to consider regarding the exit tax is the use of gifts before your expatriate to reduce your net worth. Under the December 2010 tax agreement between the President and Congress, each individual has a $5 million lifetime gift exemption. With proper planning, you can take advantage of gifting to reduce your exit tax liability, and possibly even lower your net worth below the threshold so that the exit tax no longer applies to you. [Note that both the estate/gift tax as well as the expatriation tax are highly politically contentious issues in the U.S. and could change at any time, so you should definitely confirm that the law which would apply to you is currently as we describe here].

Resident Non and Citizens

Since resident and nonresident aliens are taxed differently, it is important for you to determine your status. You are considered a nonresident alien for any period that you are neither a United States citizen nor a United States resident alien. You are considered a resident alien if you met one of the following two tests for the calendar year:

The first test is the "green card test." If at any time during the calendar year you were a lawful permanent resident of the United States according to the immigration laws, and this status has not been rescinded or administratively or judicially determined to have been abandoned, you are considered to have met the green card test.

The second test is the "substantial presence test". For the purposes of this test, the term United States includes the following areas:

- All 50 states and the District of Columbia
- The territorial waters of the United States, and
- The seabed and subsoil of those submarine areas that are adjacent to U.S. territorial waters and over which the United States has exclusive rights under international law to explore and exploit natural resources.
- The term does not include U.S. possessions and territories or U.S. airspace.

To meet the **substantial presence test**, you must have been physically present in the United States on at least 31 days during the current year, and 183 days during the 3 year period that includes the current year and the 2 years immediately before. To satisfy the 183 days requirement, count all of the days you were present in the current year, and one-third of the days you were present in the first year before the current year, and one-sixth of the days you were present in the second year before the current year.

Do not count the following days of presence in the United States for the substantial presence test:

- Days you commute to work in the United States from a residence in Canada or Mexico if you regularly commute from Canada or Mexico. You are considered to commute regularly if you commute to work in the United States on more than 75% of the workdays during your working period.
- Days you are in the United States for less than 24 hours when you are in transit between two places outside the United States.
- Days you are in the United States as a crew member of a foreign vessel engaged in transportation between the United States and a foreign country or a U.S. possession. However, this exception does not apply if you otherwise engage in any trade or business in the United States on those days.
- Days you intend to leave, but could not leave the United States because of a medical condition or problem that arose while you were in the United States. Whether you intended to leave the United States on a particular day is determined based on all the facts and circumstances.
- Days you are an exempt individual.

An **exempt individual** may be anyone in the following categories:

- An individual temporarily present in the United States as a foreign government-related individual
- A teacher or trainee temporarily present in the United States with a J or Q visa who substantially complies with the requirements of the visa
- A student temporarily present in the United States with an F, J, M, or Q visa who substantially complies with the requirements of the visa; or
- A professional athlete temporarily present to compete in a charitable sports event

Even if you meet the substantial presence test, you can be treated as a nonresident alien if you are present in the United States for fewer than 183 days during the current calendar year, you maintain a tax home in a foreign country during the year, and you have a closer connection to that country than to the United States. This does not apply if you have applied for status as a lawful permanent resident of the United States, or you have an application pending for adjustment of status. Sometimes, a tax treaty between the United States and another country will provide special rules for determining residency for purposes of the treaty. An alien whose status changes during the year from resident to nonresident, or vice versa, generally has a dual status for that year, and is taxed on the income for the two periods under the provisions of the law that apply to each period.

If you are a nonresident alien, you must file Form 1040NR (http://www.irs.gov/pub/irs-pdf/f1040nr.pdf) or Form 1040NR-EZ (http://www.irs.gov/pub/irs-pdf/f1040nre.pdf) if you are engaged in a trade or business in the United States, or have any other U.S. source income on which the tax was not fully paid by the amount withheld. If you had wages subject to income tax withholding, the return is due by April 15, provided you file on a calendar-year basis. If the due date falls on a Saturday, Sunday, or legal holiday, the due date is delayed until the next business day. If you did not have wages subject to withholding and file on a calendar-year basis, you are required to file your return by June 15th. If the due date falls on a Saturday, Sunday, or legal holiday, the due date is delayed until the next business day. File Form 1040NR or Form 1040NR-EZ with the Internal Revenue Service Center, Austin, TX 73301-0215.

If you are a resident alien, you must follow the same tax laws as U.S. citizens. You are taxed on income from all sources, both within and outside the United States. You will file Form 1040EZ (http://www.irs.gov/pub/irs-pdf/f1040ez.pdf), Form 1040A (http://www.irs.gov/pub/irs-pdf/f1040a.pdf), or Form 1040 (http://www.irs.gov/pub/irs-pdf/f1040.pdf) depending on your tax situation. The return is due by April 15, and should be filed with the service center for your area. If the due date falls on a Saturday, Sunday, or legal holiday, the due date is delayed until the next business day.

At US-Taxman we deal with Resident and Non-Resident Aliens on a daily basis and are well equipped to answer all your US Expat Taxation questions. Please feel free to contact us.

IRS Due Date & Deadlines

Federal Tax Return Expat Tax Deadlines & Due Dates Only are Listed Below - Various states may have other filing deadlines - This only includes the most common filing dates and should not be relied on for all filing dates.

Have you estimated your 2013 tax?	If you live in a low tax country - such as Hong Kong, Dubai or Singapore - you may owe US tax. Hence you should complete making estimated payments for 2013 and get ready to start making estimated tax payments for 2014. We provide this service to our clients.
January 31	File your tax return 2013 if you did not pay your last installment of estimated taxes - this is the last chance to avoid penalties for underpayment of estimated taxes for 2013.
March 15	File form 3520-A for owners of foreign trusts (also applies to the owners of UK and Australian IRA-like accounts).
April 15	First 2014 estimated tax payment is due.
April 15	Deadline to file US Federal tax returns. If you reside outside the U.S. on 4/15/2014, you get an automatic extension until June 15. However - if you owe any tax for 2013, it is due on 4/15/2014 and interest will accrue from this date.
June 15	Deadline to file an extension for Federal Return (for expatriates only). If you need to file an extension you can visit www.officialpayments.com and file a Form 4868. If you don't expect to owe tax, simply pay $3.95 and get an extension. Cheaper than going to the Post Office.
June 15	Second 2014 estimated tax payment is due.
October 15	Final due date to file calendar year 2014 tax returns for taxpayers who received a 6-month expat extension
October 15	Third estimated payment for 2012 due date.
December 15	Final date to timely file tax return for 2013 for expats who requested an additional 2-month extension.

If you owe money to the IRS, you might be wondering when it's due (especially with the filing extensions granted you as an expatriate). It's easy to be confused, as an expat, about the deadlines for U.S. taxes. In this article we will cover the deadlines for tax returns and FBAR forms, as well as how to file for an extension if needed.

Regular Tax Filing Deadline
All Americans know "tax day" as April 15th. And while this is normally the case, the tax filing deadline will be pushed to the following Monday if the 15th falls on a weekend or a holiday. The filing deadline for the 2011 tax year is April 17th, 2012.

Federal Expatriate Extension, When and How it Applies
As an expat, your necessary tax documents may arrive at different times than you were accustomed to in the U.S. To accommodate you, the IRS automatically extends your filing deadline to June 15th of every year. This automatic kindness does not extend to money owed, however. Any money you owe the IRS will still be due on April 15th (or the following Monday if April 15th lands on a weekend or a holiday). In other words - you are allowed an automatic **2-month extension to file your return and pay federal income tax** if you are a U.S. citizen or resident alien without **incurring late penalties**. Even though you are allowed an extension to file, you will have to **pay interest** on any tax not paid by the regular due date of your return (ie April 17th in 2012).
Any payments made **after June 15** would be subject to both **interest charges** and **failure to pay penalties**. Without filing, you may not be aware of how much money, if any, you will owe. Regardless, interest on money owed will begin to accrue as of April 16th (or April 18th in 2012). If you expect to owe money to the IRS, it is wise to file as early as possible to avoid a higher payment at a later date.

Your first quarter estimated tax for 2012 is also due to be made on 4/18/12 using form 1040 ES. Please note that underpayment of estimated taxes by as much as $1,000 or more for the year will generate the underpayment penalty - even if all payments were made on time. If your self-employment income exceeds your previous year income by more than 10%, contact your tax advisor to revise the estimated payment amounts.

You can extend until 10/15/12 your expatriate tax return on or before 6/15/12 by filing Form 4868 with the appropriate box checked. If you need to extend your expatriate return beyond that date in order to qualify for the foreign earned income exclusion you need to file Form 2350.
If you do not file the necessary form to extend your personal return and end up owing taxes, failure to properly extend the form will result in the large penalty of 5% per month of the tax due up to a maximum penalty of 25% of the tax due plus interest. Best to not miss filing that extension due to this high penalty

Further Extension
Even with the two month extension, it is possible that your forms may not arrive in time. As an expatriate, if you find that you need more time, you can request an additional extension to October 15th. To file for this extension, simply have your accountant file Form 4868 on your behalf. You can also complete the form yourself if you choose to. However, as with all things tax related, it's usually worth the expense to hire a professional.

Filing an FBAR Form
In addition to filing with the IRS, many American expats are required to file a foreign bank account report (referred to as an FBAR) http://www.us-taxman.com/fbar.php. The FBAR is required for any expat who has over $10,000 in foreign bank accounts at any point (even one day) during the year. Anything over $10,000 (and this figure applies to all foreign

accounts combined) must be reported. The specific number of the FBAR is Form 90-22-1. This form is due (to the Treasury, the FBAR is not filed with the IRS) by June 30th; and, in the case of an FBAR, there are no extensions. Many expats falsely assume that they do not need to file an FBAR. "Foreign account" is not limited to standard checking and savings accounts, however. You must also take into account your mutual funds, trusts, and brokerage accounts. Also, your business accounts may need to be included. Contact an international tax expert if you are unsure of how to proceed. And do not put the calculating off until the last minute. If you have multiple accounts, this can be a very complicated process.

Record Retention Rules

Good recordkeeping can cut your taxes and make your financial life easier.

How long to keep records is a combination of judgment, state, and federal statutes of limitations. Since federal tax returns can generally be audited for up to three years after filing and up to six years if the IRS suspects underreported income, it is wise to keep tax records for at least seven years after a return is filed. Requirements for records kept electronically are the same as for paper records.

Generally, follow these recommended retention periods for various documents:

Record	Retention Period
Tax returns (uncomplicated)	7 years
Tax returns (all others)	Permanent
W-2s	7 years
1099s	7 years
Cancelled or substitute checks supporting tax deductions	7 years
Bank deposit slips	7 years
Bank statements	7 years
Charitable contribution documentation	7 years
Credit card statements	7 years
Receipts, diaries, logs pertaining to tax returns	7 years
Investment purchase and sales slips	Ownership period + 7 years
Dividend reinvestment records	Ownership period + 7 years
Year-end brokerage statements	Ownership period + 7 years
Mutual fund annual statements	Ownership period + 7 years
Investment property purchase documents	Ownership period + 7 years
Home purchase documents	Ownership period + 7 years
Home improvement receipts and cancelled checks	Ownership period + 7 years
Home repair receipts and cancelled checks	Warranty period for item
Retirement plan annual reports	Permanent
IRA annual reports	Permanent

IRA nondeductible contributions (Form 8606)	Permanent
Insurance policies	Life of policy + 3 years (Check with your agent. Liability for prior years can vary.)
Divorce documents	Permanent
Loans	Term of loan + 7 years
Estate planning documents	Permanent

Don't wait file now!

The Author: Dan E. Gordon is:

http://www.us-taxman.com

dan1@us-taxman.com

US Taxman is a full-service Tax Preparation and accounting firm

The US Taxman staff enjoy the work they do from the simplest 1040EZ to the most complex corporations, with the goal that no client should pay more tax than legally required.

Please free to call and talk to our friendly staff and make an appointment to begin building a solid understanding of your taxes and a strong financial future. We look forward to serving you and developing a personal working business relationship for years to come.

US Taxman
Bangkok:089-521-0941 * 06-003-55800 * FAX:02-741-7755

Please be aware that our office hours are:
9:00 AM to 5:00 PM - GMT +7 (Bangkok time) * Monday - Friday
US Phone: (253)220-2061 * FAX: (206)350-8089
Tokyo: (81)3-5501-1270 * Hong Kong: (852)3693-1503
Singapore: (65) 3108-0290 * Paris: (33)17-999-3180
Germany: (49)69-2222-7566 * London: (44)208-819-4103
Malaysia: (60) 3-2788-4796 * London: (44) 203-455-5002
Skype us-taxman